THE RED BOOK
AND THE
GREAT WALL

The Red Book and the Great Wall

An Impression of Mao's China

Alberto Moravia

Translated by Ronald Strom

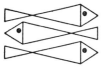

FARRAR, STRAUS & GIROUX
New York

CONTENTS

THE RED BOOK
AND THE
GREAT WALL

INTRODUCTION

B: So you have been to China?

A: Yes, I have been to China.

B: What impressed you most in China?

A: The poverty.

B: The poverty?

A: Yes, the poverty?

B: Are the Chinese poor?

A: By Western standards, very poor.

B: What impression did their poverty make on you?

A: Relief.

B: Good Lord! As far as I know, poverty means degradation and frustration. And instead you felt relief. How is that?

A: I felt it, I am sure of that: one can't mistake one's feelings. I felt it the whole time I was in China. But you ask why I felt it. I hadn't thought about that. I'll try to think about it now and give you an answer.

B: In the Western world poverty does not inspire relief. On the contrary. It inspires a sense of oppression and a will to revolt. Look at the American Negroes, for example, burning their ghettos.

A: In the United States there are poor people and there are rich people. The poor people are poor because there are rich people, and the rich people are rich because there are poor people. In China there are only poor people.

B: I see. Everyone is poor in China. I should have thought of that.

A: Yes, everyone. But to call them poor is inexact. One ought to call them something else.

B: For example?

A: I can't give you an example. No word exists yet to describe a poor man in his own terms, without comparing him with a rich man.

B: What, in fact, is Chinese poverty then?

A: I would call it a poverty without wealth. That is to say, if you look closely, the normal condition of man.

B: Explain yourself.

A: It's quite simple. Man is born destitute of everything, naked as the beasts of the forest. At birth man is not yet a man. To become one he must provide himself with the things that make man a man. In other words, with that which distinguishes man from animal. And that is because man is almost entirely an animal like all the others, to such a degree that one often wonders if it was worth the effort to become man. Now what is necessary to become a man is within the limits of poverty; rather, it is poverty itself, nothing more and nothing less. Beyond this limit begins wealth, which is to say, the superfluous. But poverty is man's normal condition, because wealth, which is superfluous, does not make him more a man than poverty does.

B: To be rich then, according to you, would be an abnormal condition for man?

A: Abnormal, hence inhuman.

B: In what does this inhumanity consist?

A: It consists in attributing an expressive function to everything that is superfluous.

B: Isn't the superfluous expressive?

A: Obviously not. Otherwise it wouldn't be superfluous.

B: Tell me, when is it that man goes beyond the necessary, that is, the human, and enters the superfluous, that is, the inhuman.

A: Let's look at China again. The Chinese, judging from what one can see on the streets, possess the necessary but not the superfluous, at least for now. They are poor, as I've already said. No one could doubt that their humanity is complete, but it lacks something that could be obtained through wealth, that is, the superfluous. I was in China thirty years ago. Then there were poor Chinese who had barely enough and rich Chinese who lived on the superfluous. The former were degraded and the latter were inhuman. As soon as the rich and their superfluity disappeared, the poor suddenly became human again, although they still had only barely enough.

B: Still there is something cheerful, gay, and vital about abundance. Your "necessary" may be human, I'm not saying it isn't. But it is sad.

A: There is no abundance in the modern world. There is production, which is not cheerful or gay or vital.

B: What is the difference between abundance and production?

A: Abundance is a gift of nature that does not cost labor, money, or time. It is not intended for consumption but for the imagination. Production, instead, costs labor, time, and money, and therefore it is never abundant. It is simply repetitive, that is to say, it consists in the multiplication of a single product for greater consumption.

B: That may be. But you will admit that the Chinese, if you were to tell them that their poverty is the normal condition of man, might also protest. Probably most of the Chinese want to be less poor or—within the limits and means of Communism, of course—even rich.

A: You may be right. But I am talking about China as it is now, formulating the risky hypothesis that it will not change. In other words, for me China today is a utopia that has been achieved, perhaps involuntarily, perhaps by chance, it makes no difference. It is achieved and I take it as an example in my argument. Later, perhaps, China will become a country like all the others, including the Communist countries of the Soviet persuasion, in which there are the poor because there are the rich and vice versa. But for now, today, China is a poor country without rich people, that is, a country in which poverty is synonymous with normalcy.

B: I see. So production and consumption beyond what is necessary are inhuman. But who is to decide what is necessary to man and what is not?

A: Man himself. In other words, common sense.

B: There have been periods in history in which to be a man one had, above all, to possess and to display the superfluous. The Renaissance, for example. What do you say to that?

A: I say that periods in history do not interest me at all, nor does history in general. What interests me is the present.

B: Let's talk about the present, then. I repeat: who is to decide where the necessary, or human and normal, ends, and where the superfluous, or inhuman and abnormal, ends?

A: I've already told you. Common sense.

B: You have great confidence in common sense.

A: Yes, I believe in the common sense of common people. Which, as far as the things of this world are concerned, is not as much a question of intelligence as it is—how can I say it?—a question of hunger and lack of appetite, of amusement and boredom, of desire and gratification, and so on. One day common people, endowed with common sense, are going to get bored with being inhuman or, rather, with being continually dehumanized by wealth. And then they will get rid of it, even if philosophers and producers of the superfluous swear that they are wrong.

B: How will common sense act in the face of wealth? That is, how will common sense manage to get rid of wealth?

A: In the face of wealth, common sense will act somehow automatically. Having reached the acme of inhumanity, man will want to, and will, become poor.

B: Automatically? Man's automatisms are actually long, tortuous, difficult, and costly processes.

A: It will be a human process. Man is slow.

B: And what will man do to become poor again, after having been rich?

A: He won't do a thing.

B: What does that mean?

A: It means that he will not consume, and consequently will not produce, more than the necessary.

B: But man loves to produce and he loves to consume.

A: What man?

B: Man. Man in general.

A: I know nothing about man in general. Man today, yes—as you say, he loves to produce and to consume. But the man of tomorrow might be completely different.

B: Let's get down to the concrete. Let's talk about real wealth and poverty, as one can see them in the world today. Where is the most human poverty today?

A: In China, in my opinion. In China, now, at this very moment, I mean. There is no certainty that China wishes to or can transform into an enduring reality the utopia that it temporarily embodies and represents today. In other words, it is not at all certain that the Chinese situation of tomorrow will be like that of today. In order for utopias to stop being utopias and to become realities, they must last.

B: Now tell me, where is the most inhuman wealth today?

A: Today, in the West, in my opinion.

B: Let's take things in order. First of all, let's talk about China. Let us suppose that the Utopia of Poverty, as you call it, becomes permanent, that it is transformed, to use your own words, into an enduring reality. How will the Chinese achieve this result?

A: They must simply continue to do what they are doing now.

B: But you know very well that the Chinese must transform China from a peasant country into an industrial country. So their poverty is nothing but the normal result of the capital investment required to complete the industrial revolution.

A: I know that. The Chinese are doing today what the Russians did forty years ago and the West a century ago.

B: Now let us suppose that the industrial revolution is achieved, that ever larger profit margins are accumulated, and that investment becomes continually less necessary. What will the Chinese do then with this capital that will continue to accumulate? They will have to increase wages and create light industry and consumer goods, so that wages can be spent. And there you are, China will become a country like any other; it will become rich.

A: Yes, that's true. But you forget that we were talking about utopia. There is a utopia in China or, rather, there is an attempt to transform utopia into history. Utopia obviously leads to utopian solutions.

B: I really would be curious to know what utopian solutions China could find in order to remain poor even though rich.

A: First of all, utopia must become conscience. Once this conscience has been created, the solution will be to make wealth feel sinful, guilty, criminal.

B: Christianity tried that, without, I should say, achieving encouraging results.

A: Nevertheless, Christianity managed *for a few centuries* to exalt poverty as an ideal state. Even today this would be a considerable achievement. For you must remember that I am not speaking in absolute terms but relatively, not outside space and time but in relation to the time and world in which we happen to live. Yet I have to admit that the mark of failure is clearly evident in the adjective "ideal," which defines the condition proposed by Christianity. No, this time it won't be enough to advance poverty as an "ideal state." Instead it must become the sole, real, normal state of man.

B: And how is all this going to come about?

A: For the first time in its all too short history, mankind will have the chance to be totally rich, to enjoy all that is superfluous. Not just a part but all mankind this time will know what it is to be rich. So that when all mankind has tasted the inhumanity of wealth, it will with the same unanimity desire to be poor.

B: Let's accept that for the moment—although, at least for now, two thirds of mankind not only are far from being rich but are so poor that they do not have enough to eat. But let's accept that. Wealth will then be considered sinful, guilty, criminal. But there will still be wealth, albeit in state treasuries. What will happen to it?

A: I've thought of that. Have you ever heard of the Pharaohs?

B: How do the Pharaohs come into this?

A: Have you ever asked yourself why the pyramids are so large and cost so much time, so much labor, so much money?

A: Let me hear, why?

A: Because, in my opinion, it was necessary that man have nothing but what was essential. Everything else was destroyed. The pyramid in peacetime is what war is in wartime. Something that serves to destroy wealth and keep man in poverty.

B: But where are our pyramids?

A: Our pyramids are scientific projects for the conquest of Mars or Venus or the moon, for travel through cosmic space. These scientific projects, because of their inordinate expense, the vast number of men they employ, and the enormous toil they involve, are the exact equivalent of the pyramids. Besides, the pyramid was not the absurd caprice of a despotic theocracy. It was the pivot, the center of a complete civilization. In the same way that our interplanetary flights are today.

B. But the United States, to take an example, makes war and at the same time has its pyramids, that is, its projects for interplanetary conquest, and it is still rich.

A: The United States is "provisionally" rich, as China is "provisionally" poor. And as I have used China as it is today as an example of poor, that is, normal and human, mankind, so I will now use the United States as an example of rich, that is, abnormal and inhuman, mankind.

B: The United States or the West in general?

A: The United States as a typical Western country. Actually, the West.

B: Don't you think that the West will always be rich?

A: Certainly not. In fact, it is doing everything needed to become poor. But let's put the future aside. Let's stick to the present. Let's see why wealth is inhuman and abnormal.

B: Let us, indeed!

A: Take any individual who wants to become rich by inventing something new and absolutely superfluous. For example, a shoe that plays music at every step when one is walking. What will the inventor of a shoe like that do to mass-produce his product and sell it to the general public?

B: I don't know. Publicity, I imagine.

A: Right, publicity. In other words, he will create a demand for musical shoes, a demand, by the way, that did not exist until the shoes were put on sale. No manufacturer, however, is ever going to say: "I am selling you something you don't need." He will always say: "I am selling you something you cannot do without." Now, this transformation of the superfluous into the necessary is what creates the so-called consumer.

B: There are consumers everywhere. Even a Chinese, when he buys a pair of trousers, is a consumer.

A: No, he is not a consumer. He is a man who buys a garment that is necessary, according to a certain idea he has of man—a garment to cover his legs, his belly, his seat, and so on. A consumer is merely a gut.

B: What are you saying?

A: I am saying that the consumer is a gut. That is, a creature similar to those very simple organisms that have only mouth, intestines, and anus. These organisms do nothing but ingest, digest, and discharge.

B: But the Chinese consumer of the trousers is also a gut, at least as far as the production of trousers is concerned.

A: There is a difference. The consumer is a gut not so much because he consumes as because he is convinced, like those simple organisms, that his function is to consume. The Chinese, poor fellow, buys his trousers, on the contrary, so as not to be naked. In short, the consumer is ready for any kind of consumption in the same way that the earthworm is ready for any kind of earth to pass through his intestinal tube.

B: And that's a consumer? A worm?

A: If the words "gut" and "earthworm" bother you, for whatever moralistic connotation they seem to have, let's just say that the consumer is merely the missing link between production and consumption. A human link, yet nothing more than a link. Likewise, the producer is the link between consumption and production. Producer and consumer then represent one the forward extremity and the other the posterior of the same earthworm.

B: Producer and consumer, nothing else? Not doctor, artist, laborer, peasant? Nothing else but producer and consumer?

A: The words "production" and "consumption" cover all products and their sale, even the most cultivated and extravagant.

B: So that Western man thinks of nothing but producing and consuming?

A: That's right.

B: And he does not think of himself?

A: This self you speak of does not exist. Or rather it only exists in the alternating periods of production and consumption. But since, fundamentally, it is consumption that characterizes the consumer (there doesn't exist a producer who does not consume, otherwise he would die of starvation; but the consumer who does not produce does exist—and how!—in every country, be it capitalist or Communist), let's just say that the end of modern civilization is consumption, that is, excrement.

B: Excrement?

A: Excrement. In other words, the discharge from the body of everything that remains after digestion. One consumes all one can and in the greatest variety: the

consumer's ideal is consumption and he strives to live
up to his ideal. But the final result is excrement. Consumer civilization is excremental. The amount of excrement discharged by the consumer is actually the best
proof that the consumer has consumed.

B: All right. It's a metaphor, and in dubious taste as
well. It remains to be seen if it can be extended beyond
its literal meaning. There are other things besides food-
stuffs in this world.

A: The metaphor is equally valid for everything that
is not properly speaking aliment but is nevertheless consumed. Above all, it is valid for industrial production
in general.

B: And how is that?

A: In modern cities production and consumption, that
is, industrial aliment and its residual excrement, are
always in close proximity just as in modern houses the
kitchen is often next to the bathroom. Go outside the
center of cities. You'll see the factories with their huge
sheds and their blast furnaces where goods are produced. And not far from the factories the bleak terrain
where the refuse, detritus, and scrap is dumped. The
city has consumed the product, digested it and defe-
cated the rest.

B: There isn't just industrial production in a large
modern city. There are many things; culture, for example.

A: Certainly there is culture. Bookshops, newsstands,
films, television sets, radio. Condensations of books,
illustrated magazines, pocket books, encyclopedias, an-

thologies, popularizations, translations. But this culture is consumed in the same way that industrial products are. It is ingested, digested, and discharged in an immense quantity of excremental commonplaces. The omnivorous consumers of culture are not nourished by culture. They consume it and remain, in a cultural sense, perpetually undernourished. Cultural consumption produces nothing but cultural excrement, nothing else.

B: But don't you think that this is all a bit—how shall I say it?—schematic?

A: That it is, certainly. But so is the modern world of production and consumption. Behind an apparent variety is hidden a single idea or, rather, a single motive.

B: What is that? The idea of profit?

A: No, it's not the idea of profit. It's something different. A new idea or, rather, a new motive that didn't exist before.

B: You're arousing my curiosity. What is it?

A: In a very rapid circulation of money like that which accompanies the production-consumption cycle, profit is secondary: it is no longer an end but only a means of assuring the continuity of the cycle. No, it is not profit that is at the origin of the excremental machine of consumption industry, but something else.

B: What?

A: It's hard to define. One might call it a will to potency. Actually, it would be closer to the truth to call it fear of impotence. What is potency in industrial civilization? It is the productive faculty, that is, fundamentally an aping of nature. Nature is potent inasmuch as it produces ceaselessly and limitlessly; natural man is potent inasmuch as he is prolific. Thus potency in a civilization of production and consumption will consist, of course, in producing as much as possible. In this sense the productive process takes precedence over the process of consumption. It is evident, however, that without consumption there could not be production.

B: What does this mean? That industrial civilization is competing with nature?

A: Yes, that is exactly what I am saying. The fear of impotence and the satisfaction of potency that drive an automobile manufacturer to produce ever greater numbers of cars ultimately share the same blind creative impulse that every year makes the sardine lay millions of eggs, that is, bring into the world millions of potential sardines. Fortunately the eggs are consumed by other fish, who, in turn, lay millions of eggs for the consumption of other fish, and so on. Industrial civilization is an exact copy of this incessant productive process of nature. And, like nature, it tries to get outside of time, outside the measure of human life, by a perpetual alternation of production and consumption, which is basically the equivalent of natural eternity. But there is a difference between industrial and natural eternity.

B: What is this difference?

A: Nature doesn't know what it is doing and perhaps for that very reason does it well. Industrial civilization, however, has a moment, only a moment, of awareness, and that is enough to make it lose its race with nature.

B: And what is this moment of awareness?

A: It is the moment when man, the indispensable link between production and consumption, sees himself. In other words, he contemplates. And refuses the eternity that industry offers him.

B: Is the consumer capable of this?

A: The consumer is also a man, after all. And he has the contemplative capacity of man. He sees himself . . . and realizes that, while it is right that nature should produce and consume for all eternity, mankind is not bound either to produce or to consume limitlessly but rather to express itself within limits, limits established by itself, of space and time.

B: This is the difference between nature and mankind? The one produces and consumes, and the other expresses itself?

A: Yes, that is how I think it is.

B: But can't self-expression be achieved simply by producing and consuming and nothing else?

A: We've already said that industrial civilization is excremental, that its end must be excrement. Now what does man do when defecating? Express himself, perhaps?

B: No, I shouldn't say that. He relieves himself, if anything.

A: Right, he relieves himself. That is, he makes himself ready to consume again. This relief is the act of defecation. But there is also the man who produces and consumes too much—he gets indigestion. In that case

we have a purgative. War, in other words. In the production-consumption cycle war seems indispensable
and inevitable to relieve the periodic constipation of
a producing and consuming society. During a war, in
fact, the peacetime consumer is replaced by the soldier,
whose consumption is exceptionally intense, vast, rapid,
and varied. More is consumed in wartime in a day than
is consumed in peacetime in a year. Finally, the soldier,
not satisfied with consuming goods and wealth, consumes human lives, first those of his enemies and then
his own. Yes, you must not forget that the producer-
consumer, in order to be such, must also—and this is
most important—be prolific and hence homicidal. Without overpopulation there is no mass production; without mass production, no overproduction; and without
overproduction, no war. Homicide is merely the other
side of the coin of prolificacy.
B: Then war would be consumption of men, even before it was consumption of goods.
A: Right. It has also been called delayed infanticide.
But war is really consumption of men, achieved by
various means, from the bayonet to the atom bomb.
The bayonet is of course insufficient for the overpopulation of the modern world and so we have the atom
bomb. But there is no substantial difference between
the two weapons, only a difference in consumptive
capacity. Moreover, the bomb is bound to overpopulation and overpopulation to the bomb. What I'm trying
to say is that if there were not overpopulation there
would not be a bomb. It would not have been invented,

because there would have been no need for it. The bomb is born the moment there are metropolises of five, ten million inhabitants, not before. Between overpopulation and the bomb there is—how shall I put it?—a kind of harmony, almost a mutual attraction. The large metropolises of the world are there, offering the largest production of men that has ever existed in history. And the bomb is there too, the only possible consumer of such gigantic production. It seems inevitable that at a certain point production and consumption meet and together, in love and concord, resolve their problems. Basically, the bomb is Malthusian. Malthus foresaw famine as the corrective to overpopulation. But Malthus was thinking in terms of preindustrial civilization. He did not foresee that man would soon cease to be the center of the universe, that man would become, as we have said, nothing more than the link between production and consumption. Today I think he would readily agree that, as a consumer, the bomb is preferable by far to famine.

B: Excuse me, but at this point there is something I do not understand. I should say that man is, in any case, prolific. He is so just as much in humanistic civilizations based on man as he is in modern civilization based on production and consumption. You are right when you say that if there were not prolificacy there would be no mass production, and, in consequence, the incessant, obsessive cycle of production and consumption would not exist. But man has always been a producer and therefore a consumer of men—even when he was not yet a producer and consumer of mass-manufactured wares.

A: The demographic pressure of the ancient world was not like that of the modern world. It developed entirely on a natural level, like that of animals. It was in response to the exceptional production of men that nature, not man, defended itself by equally exceptional consumption, in other words, by famines and epidemics. And wars too were a consequence—a natural consequence, one might say—of famines and epidemics. In the modern world, on the other hand, everything develops on an industrial level, even man's prolificacy. It seems to me that there is a very close relationship today between demographic pressure—the fact that man is a producer of men as well as goods—and the pharmaceutical industry and hospital organization. The production of men, however, does not take place so much in the dark blind intimacy of the conjugal bed as it does, later, among the white coats of doctors and nurses, in clinical wards and operating rooms. It is in those places, so like efficient factories in their mechanical perfection, that man becomes a producer of men. Not at home in his own bed. It is in those places, in fact, that future consumers and future producers are saved from the death that unjust and provident nature has destined for them. Clinics and hospitals turn out men the way factories turn out canned goods or automobiles.

B: So you maintain that modern man is already, fatally, only a producer and consumer of goods and men?

A: Yes.

B: Am I right in thinking, from the way you speak, that this makes you unhappy?

A: Yes.

B: What solution do you propose then?

A: I can see but one solution. Only one, at any rate, that depends directly on man.

B: What is that?

A: Chastity.

B: Chastity? A bit drastic as a solution, don't you think?

A: Yes, chastity. Poverty and chastity, if you think about it, are the two normal conditions of man, or at least they ought to be in the world today. For in the world today I don't see how man can cease to be a producer-consumer if not through poverty and chastity.

B: If I have understood, the poor man does not consume and therefore has no need to produce. The chaste man, for his part, does not bring children into the world and therefore, in the final analysis, discharges consumer civilization of its specific content, that is, the necessity of satisfying the needs of the masses. No children, no masses; no masses, no production and no consumption. Right. Too right, in fact.

A: You have got my meaning precisely. Note, moreover, the similarity between the process that leads to overproduction and that which leads to overpopulation. Substitute for the machine tool, mother of machine parts, the likewise mechanical embrace of the human couple in bed and you have the mass-produced product manufactured in exactly the same way. Where is the difference? In the dark, by two people in a state of semi-consciousness between sleeping and waking, a human being is conceived. At the same moment in a thousand factories, in a deafening din, provision is being made to mass-manufacture, for the being who has just been conceived, the thousands of products he will be made to consume as soon as he is born, as he grows, as he becomes an adult. Soon, however, very soon this man will become a producer as well as a consumer. He has come full circle. Let the production of men be lower than the production of goods and you have overproduction. If the situation is the reverse you have overpopulation. Only chastity can break the cycle, do away with overpopulation and overproduction, with their noisy entourage of war, famine, misery. Only chastity and, of course, poverty.

B: You are forgetting that the couple you described with such unjustified antipathy were, in conceiving man ordained to produce and consume, performing that divine and obscure thing that is the act of love.

A: Why talk of love when in fact it is really a mechanical relationship? The male member advances and withdraws like a piston in and out of the female organ. At a certain degree of excitation provoked by rubbing, sperm is discharged and the child is conceived. What has this to do with love?

B: Those two loved each other. They might have loved each other. What do we know about it?

A: Love does not lead to sexual relations. It leads to chastity.

B: That I didn't know. It's the first time I've heard it.

A: Here and now, in this world, of course. The past and the future do not concern me. They don't interest me.

B: Explain. I don't understand.

A: Here and now, in the world of today, love and the sexual relationship are foreign to each other. They are opposed and inimical. The sexual act has become nothing but production. Love, on the other hand, is love. That is, invention, a seeking, illumination, divination, identification, imagination, contemplation. Everything, in short, except production.

B: The sexual act is not merely an act of production as you believe and keep saying *ad nauseam*. More often it is performed by a man and a woman to obtain mutual pleasure. Now, eroticism is unproductive. And in some instances it can even be a means to knowledge.

A: Would that it were. Certainly it was in our archaic, primitive, magical past. But today it is nothing but a productive operation, albeit with the product removed. I mean that today the pleasure the man and woman provide for each other has no cognitive scope. As a matter of fact, it is not fundamentally different, except in appearance, from prostitution, which is clearly a form of consumption.

B: Pity! I would have been glad to see you make an exception for eroticism with aspirations to knowledge. In any case, this chaste, poor man that you predict will be threatened by rapid extinction. No production, no consumption, no procreation . . . mankind will disappear very quickly.

A: I am not saying that mankind must disappear, although today it is hard to see any reason why it should continue to exist. I am saying that it ought to—how shall I say it?—be deflated, reduced, pass from its present plethoric condition into an essential dimension. Besides, once it reached the brink of extinction, mankind, thanks to the very love it had almost abolished, would readily recover other, new reasons for multiplying again. Human things, like the things of nature, do not proceed in a continuous progression of cause and effect but in qualitative leaps. I see nothing improper in a civilization of overpopulation and overproduction being followed by one with the opposite characteristics.

B: Here I would say you are falling into the "already said." There have been many before you who have proposed a new Middle Ages. In the end it was no more than an aestheticist and decadent reversal of industrial civilization.

A: Why look to the past? No Middle Ages. Simply a world made for men and not for fetishes.

B: But technology, so important today, does not seem to be leading to this new world. On the contrary.

A: Technology today meets the needs of the producing and consuming masses. But tomorrow it could very well change its course; it could meet the needs of scanty, poor, barely prolific human groups.

B: What? Prospero's island in *The Tempest,* with the

wise technological magician and a few beautiful young men and women without offspring strolling on deserted beaches, with heavenly music, mysterious voices, and impish invisible spirits?

A: I don't know. It's been said before: it is better to be silent about things of which one cannot speak.

B: It seems to me that we have gone a long way from China, which was the starting point of this conversation. Which, after all, is merely an introduction to a small volume on the Cultural Revolution. So what does China have to do with all this? The Chinese are poor, yes, but only provisionally and involuntarily so, as you have yourself admitted. As for chastity, well, they certainly are not chaste, at least in the sense you give the word, even if they are no longer erotic, as they are said to have been once. Rather they tend to multiply, so much so that the state discourages them from marrying before the age of thirty. What are we going to do about China, then, the excuse for this conversation of ours?

A: We're not going to do anything. I merely repeat that I have tried to explain to you and to myself the reason for the sense of relief I felt at the sight of Chinese poverty. That's all. Whether the utopia of China will last forever or is temporary and passing, that is another question. It is enough for me that it has provided the excuse for a particular discussion.

cause the Cultural Revolution has the consistency of a
reality that, before it is offered to the mind, is imposed
on the senses.

We were in the station in which we were to take the
train to Canton, the first stop on our trip. We had shown
our passports to the soldier in the khaki uniform with
the red star and badges, we had opened our cases for
the inspection of another soldier, and we had also eaten
our first Chinese meal in the station restaurant. Reason-
ably enough, we expected to leave now. What else can
one do in a station except depart? But no. As we left
the restaurant, someone beckoned with a nod and directed us toward a door. We obeyed and went into a
large room that very much resembled a schoolroom.
Several neat rows of chairs, a professorial chair, and
above that a portrait of Mao. We sat down and, straight-
away, in came four or five girls who had just served us
lunch in the restaurant. Behind them came two young
men, one with an accordion over his shoulder and the
other with a tambourine.

The girls burst in with a military step, but it was a
balletic militarism, excessive and mimetic at the same
time. They were dressed like all the women in China,
in ample blue cotton trousers and a white blouse. They
stopped in front of us. Each clutched a little red book
in her hands: the quotations of Mao. One of the girls
took a step forward and announced something in a loud
voice. Then the accordion and the tambourine started,
and the girls began to sing and dance. They moved
their legs gracefully in their enormous trousers, and

WHAT ONE SEES

As soon as we crossed the border, at Lu Wu, between the British colony of Hong Kong and the Chinese People's Republic, we realized that we were not entering a country but a situation. The country is China: flooded rice paddies sparkling in the sun, bamboo forests growing up bright green hills, yellow villages the color of dried mud mixed with straw, peasants with their trousers rolled up to the knees bending over the furrows. But this physical China of today, yesterday, and undoubtedly tomorrow seems obliterated by China the situation. A situation, by the way, that is known throughout the world as the Cultural Revolution. Why do I say that the situation obliterates the physical country? Be-they raised their bare arms elegiacally in the air. Their plump little hands waved Mao's book this way and that. Their voices were fresh, innocent, discordant, and infantile. The slight steps their feet took made me think of dance-school exercises. The music was the Chinese music of all time, a kind of melancholy counterpoint. But the voices, the dance, and the music were obviously in the service of something quite different from traditional material.

In a word, it was propaganda, but I was immediately struck by the originality of the means and the incongruity of the aim. I searched my memory for an illuminating parallel or similarity, and finally it came to me. It was rustic song, peasant dances, and the country music of certain religious festivals in Italy and elsewhere that were brought to mind by the propaganda of the Cultural Revolution. Yes, that is the way they still chant the events of the Passion in Europe—with the same fervor, the same style, the same innocence. And this, then, was the first discovery, the religious quality of the Cultural Revolution and the peasant origin of this quality.

These chants, accompanied by young girls dancing and by tambourine music, were repeated again and again during our air trip from Canton to Peking. When the dance was over, the hostesses came around the plane carrying trays with various kinds of badges, all picturing the head of Mao, and photographs of Mao in different poses, taken on different occasions. They are holy images, sacred objects and badges—there is no mistaking that. And more: during the dance all the Chinese passengers chanted the same song in chorus with the hostesses. Smiling, enthusiastic, involved, and moved. Just like in church. The airplane, then, was a flying chapel in which, amid the din of the engines and the lurches of the air pockets, a rite was celebrated. I repeat, there was no doubt about it, no mistaking it. Of course, one can refrain from attempting an interpretation of this system of symbols offered by the Cultural Revolution. But then one runs the risk of not understanding anything at all, of stopping at the absurd.

Another aspect, likewise visual and plastic, of the Cultural Revolution was awaiting us in Canton during our brief stay there before leaving for Peking: newspapers on the walls. Canton is a city of arcades, a kind of Chinese Bologna drowned in the humidity, sultriness, and delirious promiscuity of the tropics. As soon as we started walking along the crowded streets, under the dark arcades, I realized that there was something extraordinary, exceptional, excessive, something feverish about the city. I was still dazed by the flight. For a moment I couldn't collect my thoughts. Then finally I understood. All the arcades, the fronts of all the buildings right up to the second story, all the buses and cars, all the monuments—every surface, in fact, including the narrow and convex surface of telegraph poles—were covered with newspapers. Sheet after sheet covered with huge aggressive black ideograms frolicking and gesticulating. The sheets were pasted layer on layer like the Italian pastry known as *millefoglie*. Naturally

the poster newspapers attracted the attention of in-
numerable groups of rapt and curiously imperturbable
readers. The city was full of crowds of passers-by who,
without comment and without displaying any feelings
whatsoever, read the violent writings, which are usually
climaxed by enormous exclamation points. What is
written in the poster newspapers? I found out. It seems
that they contain simple or at least much simplified
things: slogans, denunciations, accusations, pronounce-
ments, definitions, incitements, down-withs and long-
lives. In other words, things that appeal directly to
feeling, that do not require interpretation and analysis
by the mind.

The poster newspapers or, rather, the massive use of
poster newspapers, is one of the great novelties introduced into Chinese life by the Cultural Revolution. In
a certain sense, even the radio, with its din and imperi-
ousness, takes second place to the poster newspaper—
which, if you stop and think, is a sign before it is a
text. In fact, by its obsessive presence, it indicates that
the masses are still at a high pitch of revolutionary fervor, that in the depths of the people the revolutionary
impetus is still abundant and violent. In short, the
poster newspaper is like the surge of lava from a vol-
cano: it indicates the persistence of the eruption. But
at the same time it is a kind of political stock exchange,
an exchange like any other exchange in this world;
hypersensitive and frenetic, it gives the masses a day-
by-day account of the ups and downs of their ideology.
Finally, at least for those who are attacked and de-

nounced, the poster newspaper undoubtedly has the menacing, unpredictable, and even Kafkaesque quality of the proscriptions of ancient Rome or the proclamations of the French Revolution before the fall of Robespierre. It is not born of, it must not be born of the rational meditation of bureaucratic organs but of the fury, the inspiration and spontaneity of the people.

After a six-hour flight we arrived in Peking. Immense, limitless, vertiginous avenues on the order of Moscow's, 150 feet wide, and flanked by almost imperceptible houses (in ancient China private citizens were forbidden to build houses taller than the imperial palaces, and these, in turn, were never more than two stories high) that disappear from sight into indistinct and luminous distances. Against the light of the sun shining in the background I could not see a single automobile, but I did see swarms of bicycles. Off in the distance, in the whitish mist, something colored seemed to light up, flutter, and move. It was a red flag, one of many that have been carried in procession in the last year or so, on the most varied occasions, from one end of the city to the other.

I stopped to wait. Soon the flag approached and I saw the parade. They were boys and girls, the Red Guards, as one could guess from the scarlet band they wore on their arms. All in blue trousers and white shirts, males and females alike, and all of them clutching Mao's little book in their hands. In front was the flag bearer with a bamboo pole stuck in his belt, then two girls carrying a large portrait of Mao in a gold frame and decorated with red festoons. Behind the portrait, in single file, came the demonstrators. This was a typical demonstration; to describe this one is to describe them all. It is worth mentioning that the style of these processions, like that of the propaganda manifestations, with their chants, music, and dance, is religious, the style of traditional peasant religiosity. Replace the red flag with the standard of a religious confraternity, and the portrait of Mao with that of a patron saint, and one can see that basically nothing is changed. The Red Guards certainly represent the most modern political movement of the Communist world, but their style cannot help but be Chinese, that is, the style of a country in which the peasants form the majority of the population.

Meanwhile the traffic light had changed to red, and the procession stopped. But another one was approaching on the right, a third on the left, and three or four others appeared in the distance. Where were these columns of demonstrators going? Everywhere: to the immense square of the Temple of Celestial Peace to join other columns, to the British Embassy to demonstrate Chinese solidarity with the Arabs, to the university to hear a speech. The schools and universities had been closed for a year and would probably be closed for another year. The Red Guards, all students, could parade and demonstrate without pangs of conscience.

However, one must not forget that the Red Guards are not casual, ephemeral crowds like those one sees in the squares of Western countries. They are something stable, irreplaceable, functional. They are, in fact, one of the most important organs of the Cultural Revolution.

And now let us stop for a brief summary. I have spoken of the Cultural Revolution but not on an ideological and political plane. I have limited myself to describing the most visible aspects of it. Even from these aspects, however, one can draw interesting deductions. First of all, the Cultural Revolution appears to have only two constituent elements, the leader and the masses. It ignores, surpasses, and avoids bureaucratic, party, and intellectual mediation; it tends, instead, to establish through the radio, poster newspapers, and demonstrations a direct and immediate relationship between Mao Tse-tung and the people. In the second place—an even more important observation—these are younger people, under thirty, and they *are* the people. That is, in order to unleash the Cultural Revolution, Mao turned to the most inexpert segment of the Chinese population, that segment least endowed with a critical sense, more violent, more inclined to reject and to destroy, and more capable of enthusiasm.

Finally—another extremely important fact—the relationship between Mao and Chinese youth is not based on the pure and simple admiration and devotion of followers for their leader, but on the book of Mao quotations, that is, on Mao's thought. Thus it is not far from the truth to say that the Cultural Revolution is, among many other things, a kind of political school, with theoretical lessons and practical exercises, in which the Red Guards are the pupils and Mao is the teacher.

THE BOOK

A book that is kept in a bookcase, that is taken down to be read and, once read, is put back on the shelf is quite different from a book that accompanies one through life. The former is a consumer object, albeit an object of intellectual consumption; the latter is, on the other hand, a substitute for conscience and at the same time the axis of a system of ritual behavior. Let's see what happens in the case of the second. "He quietly recited the office and occasionally, between one psalm and another, he closed the breviary, holding the index finger of his right hand as a bookmark . . . he opened the breviary again and recited another piece, and then reached a turning in the path . . ." This is a well-known passage from Manzoni's *I Promessi Sposi* and refers to Don Abbondio and the book that accompanied him through life, his breviary. Now, in Mao's China a man walking along with a book in his hand is the most striking and disconcerting thing about the Cultural Revolution. The man, in this case, is any Chinese who considers himself a citizen first and an individual second; that is, he is all the Chinese. The book is the little red book of the quotations of Mao. The reference to Don Abbondio does not seem incongruous: the intellectual merely reads a book, but the man of faith carries it with him.

And indeed this is the most important thing one can do with a book. In the last year or so it has transformed the Chinese into so many pupils devoted to the ipse dixit. The book is carried around to show that one has it; thus we have demonstration, rather ostentation, of the book. It is waved in the air at meetings, parades, and gatherings; thus we have exaltation of the book, or threat and challenge by means of the book. It is opened and glanced at, and thus we have consultation. It is read aloud in answer to someone, and thus we have citation, communication. Closed, it is caressed with the hand or pressed to the heart, and thus we have affection. It is held in the hand during dances, songs, and propaganda recitals, and thus we have symbolization . . . It is incredible, actually, how much a little book like Mao's can influence man's behavior.

It is a very well printed book with a red plastic cover and excellent paper. On the first page is the

motto "Workers of all countries, unite!" Then comes
the frontispiece, then a sheet of tissue to protect a
photograph of Mao, then a statement in ideograms by
Lin Piao, the present chief of the army. And finally
there is a preface by Lin Piao. Notice a significant passage in this preface: ". . . the best thing would be to
memorize some of the more important sayings for constant study and application." Memorize in order to
study and apply constantly: the didactic and normative
character of the book is underlined in this simple advice.
One does not memorize the works of Marx or Lenin,
because their works were not designed as guides to
conduct. Mao's book was.

The book consists of a selection of extracts from the
complete works of Mao. Like all the Communist leaders,
Mao has written a great deal. But, unlike other Communist leaders, he has written about everything, for in his
long career he has done everything and been everything:
politician, agitator, military leader, legislator, philoso-
pher, poet, economic organizer, and so on. He has been
simultaneously the Lenin, Trotsky, and Stalin (not to
mention the Mayakovsky) of China. So it has not been
difficult to put together a book in which, in a series of
chapters with meaningful titles, the whole life of man,
one might say, is covered. But one must not think that
Mao's book can be consulted to resolve what might be
called private questions. I have said that it covers the
whole life of man, but let me say at once that it concerns a very particular man, namely, the man of the
Cultural Revolution, for whom private, intimate, per-

sonal life must not exist. In his book Mao himself puts this kind of life under the negative heading "liberalism." The book, in short, has two functions: to guide man in his daily life and at the same time to remind man that daily life is not, and must not be, any other than political life.

Mao is a typically political and typically Chinese writer. To begin with the first characteristic, it should be noted that the book has the two requisite characteristics of a manual of civil conduct. First, it has an almost scientific authority to it, for it is not a book of propaganda, of slogans and generalizations based on enthusiasm, but rather a book of reflections and affirmations derived from experience. Second, it has accessibility, because of the extremely popular simplification of its material. Thus the book appears as the fruit of complex and long experience, and this fruit is placed within the reach of everyone. It is also worthwhile to point out the educational efficacy of such a volume, in which instruction seems to be involuntary and natural. This shows, if nothing else, that from the very beginning Mao has been a politician with the vocation of an educator.

We come now to the second characteristic of the book, that it is typically Chinese. I do not want to dwell on the down-to-earth, very Chinese affability (apparent affability) that suffuses these lessons, or on the traditional, proverbial forms of speech that adorn Mao's pages (for example, the famous "imperialism is a paper tiger"). I want, rather, to consider the complex and

significant operation that for convenience's sake might
be called "the Confucianization of Marx."

Certainly no modern thinker resembles Confucius less
than Marx does. Confucius was the bearer of a conservative wisdom; Marx, the creator of a revolutionary doc-
trine. Confucius founded a wise, pious, and reasonable
humanism; Marx's humanism is heroic, irreligious,
dramatic. Everything in Confucius reflects the order,
immobility, and clarity of a stable feudal society; everything in Marx reflects the movement and dynamism
of a world in rapid evolution. Nevertheless, in the pages
of Mao, perhaps more in the tone than in the thought,
one notes a mixture, fusion, and mutual modification
of these two thinkers of such different persuasions.
Marx's thought is not substantially changed, of course,
but slightly, almost imperceptibly, shifted from the dramatic, problematic, and dialectic plane (the plane that
is appropriate to it and to all European culture) to the
educational, normative, and didactic (which is Confucius's plane and generally that of Chinese culture).
Mao can be hard, very hard, even ruthless, but his
hardness and ruthlessness are always filtered through
didactic intent.

Still more important than the Confucianization of
Marx's thought effected by Mao is the Confucianization
that, instinctively and spontaneously, the Chinese
masses have worked on this Marxism already rendered
Chinese which is Maoism. What is involved is not an
intellectual operation, as in the case of Mao, but an
operation that is, in a generic way, religious. I have

already pointed out that for some time the little red book has been the axis of a system of ritual behavior. Now no state, not even the most tyrannical, can force an entire people to transform a book of memories and politico-military reflections into a manual of conduct: the book's acceptance by the masses has been truly enthusiastic, probably far beyond the expectations of the compilers. And we should draw attention once again to the significance of Lin Piao's advice, to memorize the book for constant study and application. As a matter of fact, this is exactly what was done for centuries with the maxims of Confucius: at state examinations, applicants were asked to complete from memory selections from Confucius. Even then it was more important, clearly, to remember than to understand; good memory was a form of intelligence. And what is the significance of this preference for memory? Obviously it is this: memory holds and preserves what is not and should not be subject to criticism and hence to change. In other words, memory is a mental process that serves to confer authority, to embalm something that should not decay.

The Confucianization of Maoism, then, is chiefly a transformation into authority, by means of memory, of a personal experience, the experience of Mao. But what does this mean if not that a traditional didacticism has been replaced by another, more modern didacticism— which, furthermore, in its own way incorporates and absorbs the immense contribution of European culture?

Mao has read Marx, of course. But it will be sufficient for the Chinese masses to read Mao.

If anything, it would be interesting to see why the Chinese masses have been so quick to Confucianize Mao's thought. In my opinion, it is here that one finds the difference between Stalin's cult of personality and Mao's. Certain aspects are identical—useless to deny that. As in Russia twenty years ago, so today in China there are statues and portraits (hideous) of the dictator everywhere. And in China, as formerly in Russia, propaganda is concerned exclusively with the chief of state. But while the cult of Stalin seemed to be centered on the dictator's person in a manner not at all impious or modern, the cult of Mao seems to have passed immediately from the person to the thought, that is, to the book, taking on the coloring of primitive and peasant religious feeling. The cult of Stalin betrayed an admiration for the exceptional man, for the demiurge, the hero; that of Mao, instead, displays a pathetic need for order, a profound yearning for an enduring order. We do not know how much this was desired and inspired by Mao. From reading the book, which is basically an incitement to permanent revolution, one would think not at all. But so it is. The Chinese masses had suffered terribly during almost a century of civil wars and foreign invasions. Who can fault them if, in part out of gratitude toward the man who has finally brought them order and unity and in part because of their ancient Confucian tradition, they have attributed to the thought of the dictator a stabilizing and religious function? There is no real contradiction between the permanent revolution preached by Mao in his book and the masses' need for stability, order, and unity. A revolution made once and for all is disturbing and upsetting, but a permanent revolution becomes something canonical, stable, habitual, and, in fact, permanent. Here one can see the great difference between Europe and Asia. Europe is the continent of unstable states, of ephemeral dynasties, of numerous revolutions. But Asia is the continent of states and dynasties that last for centuries, of single revolutions that become permanent.

WHY
THE CULTURAL
REVOLUTION

The Chinese Cultural Revolution is the most important political event that has taken place in the Communist world since de-Stalinization. It is common knowledge that in the Communist world there are various levels of economic development because of the various periods in which the industrial revolution began in different areas. Corresponding to these diverse economic levels there are, obviously, diverse levels of enthusiasm, freshness, and revolutionary romanticism. Now the Chinese Cultural Revolution not only has sensationally revealed these differences but, because of the conflict and ruptures it has provoked, also seems to have created within the Communist bloc an internal dialectic which until now not even the revolt in Budapest, or Yugoslavian dissidence, had succeeded in establishing. The fact that Soviet Russia has had a noteworthy industrial development since 1917 and that China, on the other hand, was still, in 1949, predominantly a country of peasants has suddenly appeared, thanks to the Cultural Revolution, as the main cause of the ideological conflict between China and the Soviet Union. What does this mean? It means that to explain what is happening in China today one must not look for personal and individual causes, such as Mao's age, the struggle for power, the influence of Mao's wife, etc. etc.; rather, and correctly so, one must look behind the ideological conflict for the material causes.

The personal element, however, contrary to what is generally thought, is more important in Communist countries than in capitalist countries, at least at the level of government. In the West, economic differences between countries are only mildly translated into ideologies, both because of the predominant empiricism, especially in the Anglo-Saxon world, and because the Western economies are less planned and consequently less willed than Eastern economies. It is common knowledge that the economy of Communist countries is planned, and the plans are the expression of the will of limited governing bodies or even of an isolated leader. Hence the personalized character of victories and defeats in the economic field, almost as if the development of an economy were not a collective but an individual phenomenon. In China the identification of the will of the head of state with the economic and social condition of the people is more marked, I should say, than in any other Communist country. The personal history of Mao is, as a matter of fact, indivisible from that of the Chinese revolution, to such a degree that to narrate the life of Mao, as one can see from Edgar Snow's book, is equivalent to narrating the history of the last fifty years of the Chinese people.

To understand, at least in part, what has happened in China since June 1966, one must go back to remote 1927. In general, one can say that the disagreement between Mao and the Soviet Union—which, in my opinion, is at the root of the Cultural Revolution—goes back to that year. At that time the Chinese Communist Party, which had only recently been formed, was completely under the influence of Stalin. Mao himself—who was one of its leaders—with a revolutionary innocence that was shared at the time by many in the West, probably did not doubt that the remote dictator in Moscow was somehow infallible. But Stalin, through a series of mistaken instructions and false moves resulting from an abstract and infatuated ignorance of real conditions in China, provoked a terrible political and military catastrophe. For tactical reasons Stalin at all costs wanted Mao and the Communists to collaborate with Chiang Kai-shek and the nationalist Kuomintang. Chiang Kai-shek and the Kuomintang suddenly turned on Mao and wherever possible massacred his followers. Thousands of Communists were slain in Canton, Shanghai, and Peking. Mao survived the disaster by a

miracle and with the remains of his small army under-
took the famous march north.

It is beside the point here to describe Stalin's errors
in detail. Suffice it to say that among them were two
basic mistakes that Mao certainly must have remem-
bered when forty years later he unleashed the Cultural
Revolution. The first mistake was to think that China,
in its social composition, was similar to the Soviet Union
and that consequently it had to be the laboring masses
in the cities and not the peasants in the country that
would make the revolution. The second mistake was
that, no matter how things went, everything had to be
done through party bureaucracy and by means of party
bureaucracy. What happened has already been told.
As long as Mao believed in the infallibility of Stalin,
he piled up one defeat after another. When he shook
off his awe of Stalin and turned to the peasants and the
country and, bypassing party bureaucracy and ideology,
acted directly and in person, his success was immediate. Most important of all, he must have felt that his
feet were finally on solid ground.

Obeying the Soviet Union in 1927 brought Mao misfortune; thirty years later, in 1957, challenging the
Soviet Union brought him misfortune. It is always the
Soviet Union, after all, in the adverse times of Mao's
life. What happened in 1957, that year of years? The
Great Leap Forward occurred, the attempt to transform
backward Chinese peasants into modern agricultural
workers of the Russian or American type, and to saddle
state agricultural concerns with the greater part of

steel production. I am referring here to Mao's irrational, willful, and, in a word, romantic decision to set up steel furnaces—inevitably rudimentary and unsatisfactory—in the communes or state farms. The problem was industrial competition with the Soviet Union and the West. The solution, typically Maoist, was to have steel produced not just by two or three large factories but also, and principally, by the Chinese peasant masses. Every farm was to produce a small quantity of steel. China is immense; production could not but be immense, like China itself. But, this time, turning to the masses—enthusiastic, yes, but inexpert and backward—brought disaster. Steel production fell, and because of the disorder created by so much change, agricultural production also fell.

In the face of the failure of the Great Leap Forward, Mao should perhaps have blamed himself, or, as when the fault is shared by many, blamed no one. But Mao had a different reaction. What was at the root of the error, at the root of the disaster? The fact that the Soviet Union, with whom he wished to compete, was a revisionist country, a country on the road to prosperity, that is, to capitalism.

This reflection found unexpected and bitter confirmation in the Soviet Union's behavior in the face of China's difficulties. The willful and populist romanticism of Mao found no understanding or solidarity in the Soviet Union. Right away there were admonitions and ideological insinuations. Then came Khrushchev's sarcastic public remarks about the communes and the Great

Leap. And finally—a very serious step, in fact equivalent
to an act of cold war—the sudden and complete with-
drawal of Russian technical advisers.

By these measures the Soviet Union probably hoped
to restore its own authority in China, reduce Mao to
obedience, and prevent economic development in China
that would conflict with the totality of the Communist
bloc. But Mao only saw in them the obtuse and satiated
hostility of a country headed toward prosperity for a
poor country; of a country, in Lin Piao's formula, that
was already part of the urban world against a country
that was still part of the peasant world. Thus Russia—
absurdly, but, it should be emphasized, with perfect
logic—was rejected as a Western, capitalist country.

What could have made Mao change his mind? Only
this: that the Soviet Union, the second industrial power
in the world, reduce its pace to that of China, still a
predominantly artisan and peasant country; that Russia
in revolutionary solidarity share with China its techni-
cians, its resources, its means—in short, its prosperity.
Obviously this was not possible, though Mao later considered it a logical sequence. Thus through a rationali-
zation of personal disappointment and national failure,
the Soviet Union became in Mao's eyes just another
Western power, nothing more or less.

The United States, England, France, and Germany
did not have technical advisers, political and economic
missions or interests in China, much less an element
within the Chinese party and state bureaucracy that
supported their view of the world and worked for its

fulfillment. Russia did. And that, I think, is why so many things in China are or seem to be Soviet: the many boulevards of Peking, the nineteenth-century style of the modern buildings and their interior decoration, the very mixture in everyday Chinese life of drastic austerity and popular patriotism. In the same way, there must have been many Chinese who wittingly or unwittingly believed in Soviet ideology and wished that China would imitate it and model itself on the Soviet Union. These people were excellent Communists, of course, who had always believed that Russia was the guiding state of the Communist bloc and that China was a friend of Russia. Many of them had been personal friends of Mao's since the years of the Long March and even earlier. They occupied responsible posts in the state and party bureaucracy. It was against them and against everything they were thought to represent (i.e., Soviet revisionism and Western interests and culture) that Mao's romantic and populist fury was unleashed.

Characteristically, the great purge (the Cultural Revolution is, in substance, also a gigantic purge or purification) was not carried out by a Stalinist secret police. There is no secret police in China. Moreover, inasmuch as the purge was designed to strike chiefly at the bureaucracy, one could not rely on a secret police, which basically is a bureaucracy like all the others. No, Mao on this occasion, as on many others, followed his heart, which had remained faithful, innocently and nostalgically, to the strenuous years of the civil war, and he appealed, as he had then, to the masses, particularly to the young and the very young among them. He no longer seemed to stand on solid ground, or to have the strength he had had before. But with the Cultural Revolution, through contact with the masses, he once again planted his feet firmly on the ground and recovered his strength. In one year, fifty million Red Guards surged, in a new Children's Crusade, from one end of China to the other. Millions of poster newspapers appeared. There were hundreds of thousands of parades, demonstrations, meetings. More than ten million Red Guards were received personally in Peking. And all China was turned upside down: agricultural and industrial production diminished, the state bureaucracy was overturned, party bureaucracy was destroyed. Several provinces were in the hands of Maoists; others, in the hands of anti-Maoists. And this is only a partial list of the explosive results of Mao's appeal to the masses. But the barrier of bureaucracy and the party had fallen. And, even more important, the ground had been prepared for a universal revolutionary ideology that tomorrow perhaps may be able to compete with the Soviet ideology. More important still, the foundations may also have been laid for an egalitarian and technological society in which social advancement does not come through consumption as the result of profit as in the United States, or through prosperity as the prize of power as in Russia, but through the diversity and the quality of technical capabilities—a technocracy consisting of diversely qualified cadres and working masses in which everyone is provided with the necessary but not the superfluous.

MAO SAYS SO TOO

Since the first day, I had asked to meet an intellectual, a writer, but had been told that it would be difficult: Chinese writers were very busy. Then suddenly one morning the telephone rang: the writer was waiting to meet me. Where? The lounge on my floor of the hotel.

I knew the lounge, a room in Russian tsarist, that is, nineteenth-century style: old-fashioned armchairs with linen slipcovers and lace antimacassars on the arms and back; old-fashioned lace curtains on the windows; an old-fashioned teapot of blue and white porcelain with matching cups and an enormous thermos of boiling water. From the window one could enjoy an enchanting view of Peking, green and gray: the green of trees planted in countless courtyards and the gray of ceramic-tiled roofs. And as far as the horizon there was the clearest sky of blue suffused with pink, limpid and luminous.

Here we were then, seated face to face, the Chinese writer and I. Around us were three interpreters: a young man, alert and charming; a middle-aged man with an irritating official manner; and my personal interpreter, a gaunt, fussy, sardonic intellectual type. As for the writer, he was a young man, a bit stocky and with something of the peasant about him, with a big simple face and a jovial expression. He smiled often, but then, strangely enough, the jovial expression disappeared. It was the smile of a schoolteacher, an instructor, an educated man standing before the distracted pupil or thickheaded student.

I began by asking him questions about himself. Thus I learned that he was thirty-eight years old, the son of workers, and had been born in Shanghai. He had published six novels so far, and he had written two plays as well. I asked him how many copies of his novels had been sold.

He looked at the ceiling and replied, "One, in 1963, sold 400,000 copies. The last, a million copies."

"You must have earned a lot in royalties," I remarked.

"I used to earn a lot," he said. "Since the Cultural Revolution, all of us writers have renounced our royalties."

"And how do you live?"

"We receive a salary from the state."

I asked him how long it had taken to write the novel that sold a million copies.

"I spent six months with the soldiers in a western province," he said, "and then I wrote it in two months."

"Why among the soldiers?" I asked.

"It is a novel about soldiers," he replied. "I was there to gather material and share the experiences of a soldier's life."

A bit aggressively, I said, "But good literature cannot be planned, it's not tailor-made. Literature has to be free, spontaneous, without deliberate preparation . . ."

The writer was holding the little red book of the sayings of Mao. Just as I was, as a matter of fact, and the three interpreters too. He opened it, leafed through it, told us the page, which we turned to at once, and then he read aloud: "All genuine knowledge originates in direct experience."

I realized that I must answer in the same way, with Mao. Without a moment's hesitation, I too opened Mao's book, announced the page number, and when they had found it, I read in a highly didactic tone of voice: "The fundamental cause of the development of a thing is not external but internal; it lies in the contradictoriness within the thing."

The writer was not very pleased at that. He smiled but his eyes flashed menacingly behind his glasses. He reopened the book, announced the page, and read: "We deny not only that there is an abstract and absolutely unchangeable political criterion, but also that there is an abstract and absolutely unchangeable artistic criterion; each class in every class of society has its own political and artistic criteria. But all classes in all societies invariably put the political criterion first and the artistic criterion second."

That stung me. I leafed through the book, gave the page, and read: "Works of art which lack artistic quality have no force, however progressive they are politically."

Smiling biliously, the writer consulted the book of Mao and proclaimed: "All our literature and art are for the masses of the people, and in the first place for the workers, peasants and soldiers."

After a rapid search through the book, I retorted: "We think that it is harmful to the growth of art and science if administrative measures are used to impose one particular style of art or school of thought and to ban another."

Quick, smiling, and angry, he countered by reading: "Revolutionary culture is a powerful revolutionary weapon for the masses. It prepares the ground ideologically before the revolution comes and is an important, indeed essential, fighting front in the general revolutionary front during the revolution."

Sweetly, gently I in turn replied from the book: "Questions of right and wrong in the arts and sciences should be settled through free discussion in artistic and scientific circles and through practical work in these fields. They should not be settled in summary fashion."

The writer realized that I was trying to end this pedantic, medieval duel of quotations from Mao, and all at once he fell silent and became serious, as if waiting for something. Then suddenly it came to my mind that while I displayed curiosity about him, about China, about things Chinese, he, on his part, showed none about me, about Europe, about the things of Europe. And I realized that this was very Chinese. The Chinese consider themselves self-sufficient, and they probably are. A Chinese will never show curiosity about things foreign, will never seek information, ask questions, take an interest. China is a star that rotates all by itself in its own cultural firmament. To leave this orbit and stretch one's glance as far as Europe would be like undertaking an interplanetary voyage, attempting the exploration of Mars or the moon or Venus.

The writer was silent then, and so was I. In the end I was the one to break the silence. "What do you think of Lukács?"

Shaking his head, he replied, "I don't like him, he's a revisionist."

"And Sartre?"

"He declined the Nobel Prize, and he was right to do so. But he is a revisionist too."

"Let's talk about literature. What do you think of Tolstoy?"

"There are good things, but he has the limitations of his century."

"And Dostoevsky?"

This time he stopped to think, and a feeling of aversion came over him but he could not express it. Finally he said, "He's too gloomy. He's preoccupied with gloomy things."

"Well?"

"He's a pessimist. One shouldn't be pessimistic."

"Why?"

He seemed about to make a move toward the book of Mao clutched in his hand. But he caught himself and fell silent. He did not answer.

After a moment I resumed. "Have you ever heard of James Joyce?"

"No."

"What do think about Shakespeare?"

He knew him, but he was not awed by him. He answered calmly, as if Shakespeare were a contemporary. "Shakespeare was a bourgeois writer."

"Which is to say?"

"Too subjective. We tried to give a performance of *Othello*. The actors were disturbed and upset. So was the audience. It was an audience of Red Guards. After the show, when they were asked what they thought, they discouraged us from producing the play. Too disturbing and upsetting."

"And shouldn't art be disturbing and upsetting?"

"Art must serve the masses."

"Do you like Sholokhov?"

"No, he's a traitor. And besides, he accepted the Nobel Prize."

"Pasternak?"

"He's a renegade."

"Name a writer you like."

He gave me a list of them: "Fadeyev, Gorky, Furmanov, Balzac, Dickens, Mérimée." He paused and

then added a name I couldn't quite understand. Finally
I got it—Heine. I caught the Marxist echo: Marx read,
quoted, and appreciated Heine. The writer hastily
added, "Naturally these writers shouldn't be swallowed
whole, just as they are. One has to prepare critical
editions with explanations for the people—and even
with cuts."

I continued to question him. "Is philosophy taught
in Chinese schools and universities—Plato, Aristotle,
Spinoza, Descartes, Kant?"

"Philosophy isn't taught, but the history of social
development is."

"And Greek and Latin?"

"Very little. They're dangerous literatures."

"Why?"

"Because they corrupt."

"In practice," I asked at this point, by way of sum-
ming up, "the Soviet theory of Socialist Realism seems
right and proper to you?"

"Yes." He was silent for a moment, and then he con-
cluded: "Understand that we are not against classic
Chinese literature or against ancient or modern foreign
literature. We think one should take the good and leave
the bad. In a manner of speaking, there is coloring and
there is essence in literature. One should get rid of the
coloring and keep the essence. Mao says so too."

The interview was over. We were to meet again the
next day to discuss the other arts. But literature was
the art that most clearly revealed the differences between Western culture and Chinese culture. And here

I would like to interject a few words of comment. In the first place, one must not forget that China has developed almost without interaction and relationships with Europe. Imagine that the Mayas, instead of dying out after a stupendous beginning, had evolved a consistent, complete, and complex civilization for three thousand years—and you have China. In the second place, how many European writers—not just ordinary readers but *writers*—if asked, would show any familiarity with the works of ancient and modern Chinese writers? And, finally, the politicalization of literature is a gift of the Russians. It is not a Marxist theory; it is a Soviet theory. Marx, good German that he was, respected the independence of culture. He never said that literature should make political propaganda. Stalin said it. And Stalin got the idea straight from Tsar Nicholas II's secret police, which was convinced that literature, since it was realistic and truthful, must be dangerous, and consequently persecuted the intellectuals—until the intellectuals, by dint of being persecuted, really did become dangerous, did make literature political. Then, with the Revolution, the intellectuals came to power and they demanded socialist realism, that is, a culture that was political, a culture favorable to the Revolution. China, the Chinese say, must free itself of Soviet influence. But before that, in my opinion, it must get rid of Socialist Realism, the art of propaganda.

THE BOURGEOISIE
IS THE TROUBLE

One of the fundamental ideas of the Cultural Revolution, repeated over and over again in the writings of
Mao, is that, contrary to what is happening in revisionist and neo-capitalist Russia, the dictatorship of the
proletariat (dictatorship *tout court*) will be necessary
in China for a long time to come, and consequently
the class struggle must be kept fully alive. Now, as far
as dictatorship is concerned, admittedly Mao's regime,
since it is engaged in the Cultural Revolution, can
hardly do without it. But the class struggle? One looks
around in China and is perplexed.

China today offers the impressive sight of an immense
country in which it would be difficult to activate any
kind of class struggle, for the simple reason that the
population seems to have been reduced to a single class,
the proletariat or popular class. The uniformity and

leveling of the masses is surely what most strikes the traveler in China today. One cannot sufficiently stress the apparently irrelevant fact that all the Chinese, men and women alike, dress the same. In other words, the differences between individuals and between the sexes have been done away with in the same stroke.

It is difficult to understand the enormous importance of this uniformity, except by remembering how important economically, psychologically, and culturally diversity is in the West. Just think of Western woman's desire to dress differently from any other woman, and of the industrial and social consequences of this desire. Actually, to find in Europe something similar to Chinese uniformity, one has to think of the monastic orders. The implications of this comparison are obvious.

As to the leveling, China today gives the impression of being one huge land of poverty, a proud and decent but nonetheless merciless poverty. There does not seem to be desperate want as there was in the past, but the style, color, tone, the way of life and the general outlook of poverty are everywhere. A unique kind of poverty, not just self-satisfied, but demonstrative and didactic as well—as if to say: "This is what man needs. Everything else is superfluous. Hence luxury; hence vile corruption of the Soviet or Western kind."

What does Maoist man need? He needs, it would seem, a pair of blue cotton trousers, a white cotton shirt, and a pair of sandals or slippers. He needs a bicycle to go to work, and a one-room dwelling to share with his family. He needs a limited number of consumer goods: cigarettes, beverages, soap, toilet articles, kitchen utensils, and so on. Public parks (formerly imperial gardens) to walk in, the only pastime that has not been made political. And he needs a continuous, obsessive, capillary propaganda on the thought and person of Mao carried through every conceivable media—poster newspapers, the theater, motion pictures, radio, television, painting, sculpture, and so on. In short, Maoist man is a citizen of a society that not only is classless but hasn't even a hint of classes. Why then, we must ask again, continue to keep the class struggle alive?

The word "cultural" can help us here. The Cultural Revolution, in fact, means what it appears to mean: a revolution that right from the start exploded not on the social plane—not, that is, at the level of structures—but on the cultural plane, at the level of superstructures. Let us remember that the first thunderbolt (in a cloudless sky) presaging the typhoon of the Cultural Revolution struck men of culture as early as 1965. They were bureaucrats, politicians, and intellectuals, or what are known as cadres, who were part of the municipality of Peking or the party leadership in Peking. At roughly the same time, the so-called policy of the "Hundred Flowers" was belied by other thunderbolts and excommunications hurled at such "flowers" as the films *The Life of Wu Hsiun* and *The Destitution of Hai Juei;* the artistic theories of Hu Feng: writing the truth; of Tsin Chao-yang: the broad road of realism; of Chao Tsiuanlin: the exploration of realism; and also of Chao Tsiuanlin: indecisive persons; of Cheu Ku-cheng: the synthesis of the spirt of the age; of Hsia Yen: opposition to the decisive role of the subject; and so on. The Hundred

Flowers, indeed! The whole bouquet was destroyed, and all that remained—large, immense, intrusive, exclusive—was the flower of Mao Tse-tung. The first skirmishes of the Cultural Revolution were directed against these "flowers" and against other buds of the same type. In short, the enemies of the Cultural Revolution—or the victims, if one prefers—are to be sought among the cadres, among men of culture. This negative tendency is fundamental.

The class struggle must be continued, therefore, and reinforced. "Class" loses its economic and social connotations, however, and becomes a "cultural" category. We all know that in China—and in all the Communist countries, for that matter—"cultural" encompasses not only literary, artistic, and scientific knowledge but also human behavior, public morality. Now we have it: class is a moral category.

Once the sense has been shifted from the social to the moral plane, one can immediately see how easy it is for Mao to give the revolution a permanent character and to give the class struggle a continuous development. A revolution and a class struggle that propose to reform society or the state cannot be permanent. But a revolution and a class struggle that aim at changing man can be. At this point let us note that class as a moral category implies that culture is an instrument (a weapon, says Mao). So-called vulgar Marxism has supposed that culture was a superstructure, an innocent and unconscious secretion of a class. But this mechanical determinism is not valid for Mao. For Mao, the classes coldly, consciously, cynically forge the weapon of culture with the aim of defending their interests. The bourgeoisie, coldly and fully aware of what it was doing, forged the weapon of bourgeois culture (i.e., all past culture in all countries). The proletariat must refuse this infernal weapon and make for itself, coldly and in full consciousness, an equally pointed and sharp weapon. The result of such a theory is obvious: a total condemnation of the art and thought of the past, both foreign and Chinese, and a deliberate, political orientation toward Maoist culture.

Class, then, is a moral category. In this moral category, the proletariat is the good; the bourgeoisie is the bad. Therefore, the class struggle in China today is a struggle against evil. In other words, class is not outside of and around man but inside him. It is the eternal diabolical temptation against which one must eternally struggle.

The effects of this situation are many and very important. First, if class is an inner flaw, everyone can be affected, even one's comrades-in-arms, even those who share power with Mao, even the mayor of Peking, P'eng Chen, or the president of the republic, Liu Shao-ch'i. Moreover, if culture is a class weapon, a weapon for good or evil, Western culture or what is considered Western culture must be struck down ruthlessly in all its forms. This explains the drastic and manifold nature of Chinese "austerity," which indiscriminately condemns Shakespeare and miniskirts, Chinese classics and dance-music records, Dostoevsky and silk stockings. It is a totalitarian austerity based on the very simple idea that the counterrevolution can incubate anywhere, even in a tube of lipstick. There are historical precedents:

Savonarola's Florence, say, or Calvin's Geneva. But these were small communities, not societies of 700 million people.

At this point one might ask: What is it all about? What is the purpose? The question can only be answered with two hypotheses.

The first is that the Cultural Revolution is a prelude, perhaps unconscious, to a war against the United States. In this case, having destroyed everything that is Western and having created, in opposition to American consumer civilization, the paradox of a deprived civilization, China would be in the best condition to take on the struggle. The second hypothesis is that the Cultural Revolution is basically a kind of Great Wall, despotic and nationalistic, with which—and this is nothing new in history—China wishes to close itself inside its own cultural borders for a very long time, ignoring the rest of the world and sufficient unto itself. In my opinion, the second hypothesis is the more probable. Because, if you look carefully, the Cultural Revolution seems to be chiefly an operation designed to establish once and for all a final orthodoxy. It is not mere chance that, in the rupture of the Communist world between "revisionists" and "dogmatists," China leads the latter. Paradoxically, the Cultural Revolution, with its furious and incessant movement, should create an absolute and enduring immobility. This contradiction is not new in Chinese history. Confucian social orthodoxy was also in apparent conflict with Taoist quietism and mysticism. In fact, however, they were two faces of a single culture.

THE GAS BURNER

The day's program included a visit to the statues (with no further explanation) and a visit to a factory. The statues, as I discovered when the automobile stopped in front of a portal with a triple roof turned up at the edges, were in the former Forbidden City, the dwelling of the emperors, now transformed into a public garden. We entered a very beautiful park with big leafy trees under which it must once have been very pleasant to stroll. There were the marvelous pavilions with their multicolored roofs in which life was passed among the rituals of etiquette. Now there were holes everywhere, mounds of mortar, scaffolding, and workmen. After the misgovernment of the so-called war lords and then the Japanese generals, the Forbidden City received the final blow from the recent bivouacs of the Red Guards and was being restored. There was the Winter Palace, a colossal colonnade under a massive colored-tile roof, at the top of a majestic white-marble staircase. The small courtyard in front of the palace was crowded with lines of students waiting under the surveillance of their teachers. What were they waiting for? Our guide told us. "They are waiting to see the statues."

After a long wait, we too entered. The interior of the palace had been emptied. Nothing remained but the enormous cylindrical columns and the naked floors and walls. But all around the walls ran a platform on which, in the shadow, we could make out several groups of statues. We approached. They were plaster statues painted an ugly brown color, almost life-size. Narrative sculptures: they told a story. A girl with glasses, armed with a pointer, indicated the statues one by one and explained.

What did this teacher explain? She explained the martyrdom of a peasant family in a distant western province before the revolution. One must bear in mind that in China today the peasants—that is, almost all the Chinese—have a single obsession—the landowner. Not the factory owner (industry is small and recent in China), but the estate owner, who dominated them for more than two thousand years. This is the bogy, the ogre, the number-one monster of Communist China. At performances of the propaganda ballet "The Girl with

White Hair," for example, when the landowner who has persecuted the heroine, an innocent peasant maid, is finally arrested and executed (off stage), at the sound of the shots the audience in a body leaps to its feet in frenzied applause. It is an audience of peasants who remember past outrages. For them the landowner is the devil.

Now then, in the story told with statues the religious character of the revolution in China is apparent once again. There is no mistaking it. What we saw was a Nativity scene, albeit political—a Via Crucis, albeit social and economic. And the story the girl with the pointer was telling was true. It was about a real feudal landowner who, it seems, lived with five members of his family in a palace of 180 rooms. The didactic pointer, in fact, was indicating a plan of the residence of that fortunate individual: pavilions, courtyards, gardens, a veritable dwelling of delight. But thirty years ago China was in a situation similar to Italy's at the time of the Lombards. Along with the lord's delights, the palace had dungeons (we were shown photographs) and chains (more photographs) for recalcitrant serfs. After the plan and the photographs, the girl with the pointer went on to describe the Via Crucis of the statues. The statues were fashioned in a clumsily sentimental, naturalistic, didactic style in which De Amicis and Sade joined with the unknown painters of the Stations of the Cross in Italian village churches. The peasant family was ragged, starving, downtrodden. The father was covered with rags, the mother had a baby at her breast, the children were skeletons, and the grandparents two beggarly wretches. The landowner, on the other hand, was a monster of sadism: beautifully dressed in a long gown, lounging on cushions, he haughtily shoved aside, with an overbearing foot, the rice offerings of the unfortunate family. The rice was not enough; the family must return to work, under the lash of pitiless overseers. Unable to satisfy their lord's greed, the father finally prostituted the eldest girl and, to the same end, sold the infant daughter. But the landlord was still not satisfied. Then the peasant revolted. In the last group of statues the landlord and his ruffians are struck down and slain and the triumphant peasant waves the banner of Mao.

It is pointless to dwell on the ugliness of the statues, however remarkable that is in a country like China, once renowned for the refinement and perfection of its artistic creations. At most let me stress again their rustic, Nativity style—the style of the peasant masses to whom Mao appeals directly through the Cultural Revolution. It is all too true that before the revolution the peasants, in the depth of misery and laden with debts going back generations, would prostitute their daughters and sell their children. This truth, unfortunately, has been expressed in such grossly didactic art that it ends up belying itself, and, at least for us, being completely ineffective.

The second part of our program was the factory. I won't bother to describe the factory. For the Communists, factories are a moral and political symbol of competitive progress and of the victory of the industrial revolution over the abhorred peasant and artisan society. For me, however, factories are factories, nothing more, and they are all alike, in China as in Europe. But I can say, for the benefit of Western readers and (you never know) Chinese readers, that it was a large factory, efficient and modern in every way.

After touring the factory I had an interview in the board room. I was introduced to a factory manager, a worker, a young man with a serious, and slightly threatening face, with the features of a Chinese tragic mask under a cascade of bristling hair. We had been served tea, and another worker was seated to one side ready to transcribe what we said.

I began. "What was it like in this factory before the Cultural Revolution?"

"We were run by a handful of traitors." (An official formula.)

"Who were these traitors?"

"Persons in authority who were taking the capitalist road." (Another official formula, translated immediately by the English interpreter.)

"I see. And what did you do to these people?"

"We unmasked them." (A third official formula.)

"Of course. But in practical terms, what happened?"

Silence, embarrassment. By saying that they had been supervised by a handful of traitors, that these traitors were taking the capitalist road, and that they had been unmasked, the young man apparently believed that he had expressed himself not in propaganda slogans but in concrete, realistic terms. Those formulas, meaningless and worn out, were for him the truth.

I persisted. "You unmasked them. What does that mean? That you sent them away?"

He replied ambiguously. "They went away."

"Who were they?"

"The director, the vice-director, and the other managers."

"Who had appointed them?"

"Higher authorities. The municipality of Peking."

"And now?"

"Now, from the bottom, we workers democratically appoint seventeen of our co-workers as managers and from these we select four as directors."

"Were there workers in the factory who shared the views of these traitors?"

"Yes, but we persuaded them. They admitted their errors and have been reeducated."

Always education, always persuasion, always the idea that man is primarily a student. My final question: "What effect has the Cultural Revolution had on work in the factory, on production?"

"An excellent effect. Production has increased, and everyone works with great enthusiasm."

The interview was over. Then they invited us to visit a worker's house. I hate visiting other people's houses, be they Communist or capitalist, for reasons that are not strictly personal. And propaganda seems to me the least valid reason: the visit could not but be prepared, staged, perhaps even faked. But, of course, we accepted. We went into a street flanked by two-story, red-brick, workers' dwellings. Children were playing, chasing each other, and women were bustling about. We entered the dwelling selected for our visit: two rooms, kitchen, and bath. An old man, a worker, lived there with his family. He was alone; the family was at work. We were introduced to him. He was very thin, with a charming, highly civilized, and curiously aristocratic face. His expression was both relaxed and concerned. He sat carelessly, with his legs crossed. He was wearing new clothes, Sunday clothes I would say: a blue coat closed at the neck, gray trousers, and slippers. We looked around. There were two beds without mattresses (the Chinese do without them), the blankets stretched across the wooden planks; a table; and, oddly enough, a small bookcase with five or six rows of books, tightly aligned, with ordinary paper covers, some as thick as dictionaries and others as thin as pamphlets. I asked the old man about himself.

He was an "engineer" (that is, a machine operator), he had lived and worked in Shanghai for a long time, and now he lived in Peking. This was our exchange.

"Are you still working?"

"No, I am retired."

"And what do you do?"

"For the most part, I propagandize Mao's thought in the neighborhood."

"And the rest of the time, what do you do? Do you listen to music on the radio?"

"No, I don't like music."

"Do you watch television?"

"No, I don't like television."

"Do you take walks in the park?"

"No, I don't like taking walks."

"What do you do?"

"I read the works of Marx, Lenin, Stalin, and Mao."

As he said this, he made a slight move toward the bookcase. I was perplexed. In this country in which even the Red Guards, students, do not read Marx but read only Mao, here was an old worker who read him in his leisure time. The guide interrupted. "Shall we go?"

Then the worker, with a curious gesture of friendliness, said: "Just a moment, I'd like to show them the kitchen."

We followed him. He walked slowly, an old man with little strength left in his legs. He went into the kitchen, and we went after him. It was as neat as a pin, although there were very few pots or utensils. There was a small sideboard, a small table, and a gas burner. The old worker went over to the burner, and then a curious thing happened: the reader of the difficult and obscure Marx and Lenin, of the tedious and clerical Stalin, of the moralistic, didactic Mao, showed that his pride was all in that simple gas burner. He struck a match, turned up the flame, and ostentatiously put a pot on the burner —as if to say, "Look what I have! Have you ever seen anything like it?"

I left the house with three questions spinning around in my head. Or rather, three hypotheses. The first was that the worker did not read Marx, that the bookcase had been put there to give Western visitors a certain idea of the culture of the workers. The second was that the worker did read or, rather, forced himself to read Marx, Lenin, Stalin, and Mao, though his heart was really with the gas burner, the tangible evidence of his social progress. The third was that the worker did not read Marx, Lenin, or Stalin, but perhaps only Mao, and that the gas burner, like the bookcase, was part of the propaganda act. But his trepidation and pride in lighting the burner seemed quite sincere. Ah, the heart of man is not to be plumbed. And there may be not three or four or ten but a hundred, a thousand possible hypotheses, and we shall never know the truth.

DO YOU STUDY MAO'S BOOK IN ITALY?

There were four of them facing us in the university lounge, two boys and two girls. They wore the scarlet armband of the Red Guards on their sleeves. All four were holding Mao's book in their hands. They were very young, probably all under twenty. They had a cordial, timid, yet self-assured air about them.

I asked them, "How do you feel about the Cultural Revolution?"

"It's our revolution."

"Which is to say?"

"The revolution of youth."

"So, between a wise, old man, a learned man, say,

and one of you, a twenty-year-old or even a fifteen-year-old, which would you choose?"

"One of us, a fifteen-year-old."

"Are you for Mao against the party?"

"We're for Mao against everyone."

"Have you read Marx?"

"No. We read Mao."

"Why have the universities been closed?"

"So that we can travel, come together, and see Mao. And to reorganize the courses."

"Reorganize the courses, how?"

"In the sense of making the courses political."

I looked at them as I questioned them, and thought to myself, they are children, they are babies. They are babies in their freshness, their ignorance, their innocence, and their aggressiveness; but chiefly they are babies in the candidly religious quality of their faith. Abroad they have been called hooligans and *Hitlerjugend* (in Russia), delinquents (Anglo-American rightist version), Chinese beatniks (Anglo-American leftist version), Praetorians (Formosan version), and so on. But they brought to my mind a historical comparison: the Fifth Crusade, the so-called Children's Crusade. In 1207 a fanatical twelve-year-old shepherd boy named Stephen, armed with a letter he claimed had come from Christ, managed to gather thousands of boys and girls from all over Europe. He assured them that once they reached the sea it would open before them, as the Red Sea had for the Jews, and they would walk on dry ground to Jerusalem and free it. But when they reached

Marseilles the waters did not part. What opened instead were the holds of sinister trading ships, which carried the children not to the Holy Land but to Algiers, and there they were sold as slaves.

The Red Guards are totally ignorant and they have complete faith in Mao, a wholehearted religious conviction that tomorrow might take them, innocent and fanatical, to war in a North Vietnam or a North Korea. Children, I repeat, children with a luminous poverty and an unsuspecting chastity.

"When do you marry in China?"

"As late as possible."

"Why?"

"Man must dedicate himself first to the revolution and then to his family."

I did not persist. I knew that in China, to avoid increasing the already overabundant population, people were advised (that is, ordered) not to marry before the age of thirty. And there is no such thing before marriage as that frequently total relationship which is euphemistically called an engagement in the West. China is not antisexual, it is asexual.

At that moment a young girl came in with an enormous thermos. I hoped for an invigorating cup of good tea, but I was disappointed. The poverty of the Red Guards is such that they cannot even afford a tea bag, which costs less than a penny. Instead there was the demure tinkling of cups of hot water. Many of the young people had patches on their elbows and knees— clean, well-sewn patches, but patches nevertheless.

Their clothes had been washed in soap and water, but from thousands of tiny wrinkles it was clear that they had not been ironed. This is the norm in China: no clothes look pressed, and I have seen patches on the knees and elbows even of soldiers.

I asked another question. "Is it true that you have opposed the professors and some important state figures?"

They laughed politely, sweetly, sympathetically. "Yes, but for their own good. To educate them, to teach them, to bring them back to the road of the revolution after they had started on the road to capitalism."

I wondered. The Russians and the Anglo-Saxons talk about the Red Guards as if they were juvenile delinquents or worse. Rather, they seem to me to be political Boy Scouts, children on a crusade. And since examples are always more pertinent than explanations, here is one that illustrates the curious mixture of infantilism and fanaticism of the Red Guards. It is a story reported in one of their newspapers under the significant headline: DON'T BE AFRAID TO WASH YOUR DIRTY LINEN IN PUBLIC. The story tells how the Red Guards succeeded in getting the wife of Liu Shao-ch'i, president of the Chinese People's Republic, to come outside and perform a public act of self-criticism. The operation, in the innocent and ardent prose of the newspaper, consisted in "routing the serpent out of her hole," literally forcing "the notorious number-one thief of Tsinghua University," Wang Kuang-mei (that is the name of Liu Shao-ch'i's wife), to criticize herself before twenty thousand students, professors, and workers. If there had been a secret police in China like that of Stalin's Russia or Hitler's Germany, one knows what would have happened.

Nothing is more characteristic of the Red Guards than the complicated, infantile, and, as it were, Boy Scout method that was employed. To begin with, a group of Red Guards went to the secondary school where Liu P'ing-p'ing, Wang Kuang-mei's daughter, was herself performing an act of self-criticism, and took her to a hospital. Here, by a simple argument (Are you for or against Mao?) she was persuaded to take part in the conspiracy. Meanwhile, another group telephoned Liu Shao-ch'i's house, asked for Wang Kuang-mei, and told her that her daughter Liu P'ing-p'ing had broken her leg in an accident. The mother, a clever woman, sent a trusted friend, Comrade Li, together with her younger daughter, fifteen-year-old Liu T'ing-t'ing.

When they reached the hospital, these two learned that Liu P'ing-p'ing was perfectly all right. But, with the same argument (Are you for or against Mao?), they too were drawn into the plot. Fifteen-year-old Liu T'ing-t'ing telephoned her mother: "Mother, come at once. P'ing-p'ing has a broken leg." This time "the serpent came out of her hole." Distraught, their eyes red with tears, President Liu Shao-ch'i and his wife, Wang Kuang-mei, rushed to the hospital. There they learned from the Red Guards that their daughter was all right, that it was all a plot, and that Wang Kuang-mei would have to come with them for a solemn public act of self-criticism. Furious, Liu Shao-ch'i turned his back and left. The poor mother at this point suffered a kind of collapse, deflated "like a punctured balloon." The chivalrous Red Guards, "protecting her from the indignant crowd," helped her into an automobile. There Wang Kuang-mei pulled herself together. One of the Red Guards asked her if she was frightened, and she replied, "Not at all. I was afraid for my daughter. That's why I rushed here." The result was that at ten o'clock in the morning, in front of twenty thousand Red Guards, Wang Kuang-mei, "the notorious number-one thief of Tsinghua University," was forced into an act of self-criticism. "The serpent had been driven out of her hole."

What is the moral of the story? The immediate one is that, as I have said, the Red Guards are children on a crusade. The second is that all authority (professors, superiors, party and political leaders) are as dust, except Mao. The third is even more far-reaching. Imagine for a moment an Italy ruled by a pope who disagrees with his Curia on some religious question. Imagine that some cardinals take the pope's side and others stand up against him. Imagine that the debate is extended to the whole country, that the country participates passionately, with poster newspapers, assemblies, demonstrations, parades, etc. Imagine, however, that at the same time, despite such violent disagreement, all Italians agree on the inviolability of the Church. In other words, imagine Italy split between two movements, each claiming orthodoxy and accusing the other of heresy. It all seems highly medieval. But it is evidence of the extraordinary vitality of the political struggle in China, its fertility, its inventiveness, its complexity.

There is, then, a political struggle of a religious nature in China, but it is founded on a basic political and institutional unity. The conflict concerns a simple but extremely important point: which is the more orthodox —the Russian system of party control from above or the Maoist system of leadership by the masses from below? That's all there is to it. One might well ask why Mao, who has the power to do so, doesn't arrest his opponents (beginning with Liu Shao-ch'i), try them, and execute them as Stalin would have. But Mao is not Stalin. Mao does not want personal power based on violence, as Stalin did. Mao the educator, Mao the dialectician wants ideological power based on persuasion and education. He does not want Liu Shao-ch'i killed. He wants him to change his stand, to realize that he is a heretic and abjure his heresy.

What is involved, then, is not a struggle for personal power on the order of Stalin's but a struggle for orthodoxy of an ideological and religious order. In my opinion, the practical outcome will be either that Liu Shao-ch'i will abjure and will remain president or that he will not abjure and still remain president till the end of his term, unless he resigns first and retires to private life. I may be wrong. We may learn tomorrow that Liu Shao-ch'i is to be given a Stalinist trial and "will confess." But I don't think so.

The interview was over. We left the university and had a group photograph taken with the smiling and affectionate Red Guards. Then one of them took me aside and asked (it was the first question about Italy I had been asked in China until that moment): "Do you in Italy study and memorize the sayings of Mao Tse-tung?"

"No, we don't," I replied. "Perhaps some specialists study them. We've read the book, certainly. Various editions have been published."

He did not seem quite convinced or understanding. We got into the automobile. The Red Guards saluted us, waving the red book of Mao's sayings in the air.

THEY REJECT THE PETIT-BOURGEOIS PHASE

Khrushchev rancorously said of Mao that he was "nothing but a petit bourgeois with a peasant nature, to whom the working class and the proletariat are completely foreign." As for Mao, in a beautiful poem of his entitled "Snow" (curiously reminiscent of Villon's *Ballade des seigneurs du temps jadis*), which I read [in English] in large gold letters on an immense red panel at Canton Airport, he speaks of himself in this fashion: "But, alas, these heroes! Shin Shi-huang and Han Wu-ti lacked culture; / as the emperors Tan Tai-tsung and Sung Tai-tsu failed in literary talent, / And Genghis Khan/ the beloved son of heaven for only a day / could but draw his bow against the golden eagle. /

Now they are all past and gone; / to find men who are truly great with noble hearts / we must look here, in the present."

Who is right? Khrushchev describing Mao as a petit bourgeois of peasant origin (Khrushchev could be describing himself), or Mao comparing himself to Genghis Khan, in fact rating himself higher than Genghis Khan, because the latter, albeit a great warrior, lacked culture (read: Marxist culture)? *Pace* Khrushchev, the truer portrait is not his but the self-portrait, certainly not lacking in pride, that Mao has drawn of himself. Mao surely is not a "petit bourgeois of peasant origin," but that rare character who appears but once or twice in the history of nations and who used to be called, in stately tones, "the eponymous hero." Or, in simple terms, the man who gives his name to an epoch, to an entire aspect of a society. Mao is in his mid-seventies, and the unbridled and almost monstrous cult of personality to which he has abandoned himself in recent times, if it is not a cold political expedient, is undoubtedly a serious sign of weakness. Yet, considering his past alone, he can be compared only to figures of the stature and character of Peter the Great of Russia and Oliver Cromwell in England. Mao has in common with them his complex and tormented development, his physical courage, his military skill, his easily mythified adventures, and, finally and above all, that certain *je ne sais quoi*, enigmatic and plebeian, common and ambiguous, which comes not from talent but from nature. Mao has something else of the "eponymous hero," and that is the most interesting side of his character: it is his political and ideological creativeness. Khrushchev will have a place in history because he demolished the false myth of Stalin, but this place will necessarily be of a negative order. I believe Mao will have a positive place, not just for "national"—that is, Chinese—reasons, for having saved China from catastrophe, but for having created a new ideology capable of supplanting Soviet ideology. Let's look at the Cultural Revolution again. I have indicated earlier what its origins might have been and what its immediate results were. Now let's see what (and this, of course, is a personal hypothesis) the long-term results may be.

I do not think there has ever been, historically speaking, any movement of any kind that ever really (i.e., historically) was what it pretended to be, what it said it was and hoped to be. The French Revolution, for example, said it was many things, including the final revolution against privilege and human bondage. But, as it turned out, it was the successful, though not the final, revolution of one class, the bourgeoisie. So with the Cultural Revolution. Since it concerns China, a country of peasants, I shall use a rustic metaphor. Mao is a peasant who has planted an olive seed and witnesses (and his successors will see it ever more clearly) the growth and development, instead, of a majestic oak. Unless, of course, the seed is destroyed by the worm of World War III.

What is the fundamental goal of the Cultural Revolution? It is to make peasant China—humanly intact and

integrated, innocent and virginal—take the great leap
from rustic and artisan society to technological society
without going through the hitherto apparently unavoid-
able petit-bourgeois phase of Communism. That is,
to do this altogether new and almost incredible thing:
to combine the most naked poverty, the most strenuous
but most rational poverty, with the most advanced
technical progress. In short, to have the peasant—the
whole man of peasant society—achieve technological
liberty without paying the petit-bourgeois tax that
Russia and all the other Communist states of the Soviet
bloc are now paying.

I may be misunderstood when I speak of "the whole
man of peasant society" and the "petit-bourgeois phase
of Communism." Yet anyone can see that the prosper-
ous phase (relative and provincial) of present-day
Communism has all the limitations of petit-bourgeois
alienation. This mediocre prosperity, consisting of consumer objects of poor quality manufactured by the
state, finds its moral and psychological correlatives in
a host of small vanities, ambitions, prejudices, mean-
nesses, honors, and conventions inherent in the petit
bourgeoisie throughout the world. Perhaps this will
lead to technological civilization nevertheless. But it
will come in the tow of a petit-bourgeois mankind whose
moral progress is still to be accomplished.

The Cultural Revolution seeks to reject the petit-
bourgeois phase of Communism, the dark-suited, dark-
tied, white-shirted phase (Khrushchev went so far as
to have his clothes made by an Italian tailor). It is

striving to achieve technological liberty with the poor, patched, almost indigent, but humanly intact man that one can observe today in the streets of Peking. It is a common belief, almost an undeniable truth, that technological progress must necessarily lead to overproduction in light industry and to overconsumption of mass-produced merchandise. Yet the Cultural Revolution would give the lie to this belief, would demonstrate the fallacy of this "truth," and would achieve a highly advanced technological progress that could manufacture atom bombs but at the same time would not permit the Chinese to have one shirt or one pair of trousers more than was necessary.

One might ask: once technological progress has been achieved, once the civilization of automation has triumphed, what will happen to the immense capital produced through so much work and so many privations? The answer might be this. It will be applied first to the uses of free time, toward culture, education, and the development of man; and then perhaps to scientific undertakings—the conquest of outer space, for example. It should be pointed out once again that the utopia of the Cultural Revolution would be a futuristic science-fiction civilization inhabited by the peasant, his humanity intact, not by the damaged, amputated, prejudice-ridden petit bourgeois.

I have indicated in broad strokes what might be the long-term results of the Cultural Revolution. Strangely enough, they rather resemble what might emerge tomorrow from the cultural and technological enlightenment of the United States. In the United States too, technological liberation requires a society without prejudices of any kind, a society without distinctions of race, caste, class, or wealth. In the United States too, in fact, the younger and more creative segment of the country is trying to achieve technological civilization without the cumbrous paraphernalia and antiquated trappings of petit-bourgeois prejudices.

But let's get back to Mao and China. Mao says at a certain point in his quotations: "In any given phenomenon or thing, the unity of opposites is conditional, temporary and transitory, and hence relative, whereas the struggle of opposites is absolute." What does this mean? That Mao foresees in China a perpetual dialectic, a perpetual conflict. Now, Mao's great enemy is not the United States but fundamental Chinese Confucian conservatism. The danger is that, once Mao is dead, his thought will be embalmed and his figure deified. That the cult of personality has recently grown so gigantically in China and has been Confucianized—that is, Mao's thought has been transformed into orthodox authority—is not very revolutionary. Confucian-style conservatism has been China's calamity in the past and the cause of many of its disasters. The idea of a direct passage, without a petit-bourgeois phase, of humanly intact peasant man from rustic poverty to the rationality of technological civilization, however, is certainly what distinguishes the Cultural Revolution from all other Communist revolutions in the world.

FULLNESS AND THE VOID

During my trip to China, in addition to monuments and visits to factories and communes, in addition to conversations with people of all kinds, there was another spectacle—neither anticipated nor included in the program drawn up by the tourist office—that of the Chinese crowd.

I should say that this sight alone is worth a trip to China. Moreover, without this experience any report or information, explanation or interpretation of the Cultural Revolution runs the risk of being incomplete, if not actually false. "Take a look for yourself" is not, at least in this case, a worn-out and handy cliché. It means adding to reports and information the feeling of subjective collision with objective reality, or, if you prefer, the message or messages that things transmit directly and immediately by way of our sharpest and most accurate sense, sight.

It may be impossible to know things, but it is possible to see them. And although knowledge requires long familiarity and habit and an equally long assimilation by the memory, a glance, on the contrary, requires speed and candor. I am not speaking here of the so-called "impressions" so overindulged in by journalists, diarists, and writers about things that have been seen for a century. I should say that a glance should lead to the very opposite of an "impression." In certain favorable cultural and psychological circumstances, it would be the equivalent of an identification between the observer and what is observed. Not as much, then, a fugitive and ambiguous impression as a kind of capturing of the entire object—indeed, nothing more or less than knowledge, albeit instantaneous and unreflective.

I say this so that no one will think that I presume to know the Chinese crowd in, let us say, a traditional manner: I was in China too short a time. But I have seen it, that is certain. And perhaps, since all I could do was look at it, I did come to know it as if I had lived with it for many years. However, I will limit myself to two aspects of it, which are in a sense complementary: its violence and its impassivity.

I will begin with its violence. On my return trip, the train taking me from Canton to Hong Kong made a long stop at a small station to allow a crowd of Red Guards and peasants to stage a demonstration against the imperialism of the moment, that of the English governor of the colony of Hong Kong.

The train slowly passed under the roof of the station and stopped. We got up to watch. The platform was crammed with a tightly knit crowd. But they were not travelers, they were demonstrators. In front were the Red Guards, boys and girls wearing the scarlet band on their arms. Behind them were the peasants, men and women, young and old. All of them held red banners, portraits of Mao, and posters with anti-English slogans at the top of bamboo poles. They all waved the little red book of the sayings of Mao. I watched them through the hermetically sealed windows of the compartment. Naturally I heard nothing, but I could see everything very well indeed, precisely because I could hear nothing. In a certain sense I could see better than I would have if I had been able to hear. I saw mouths open in a bellicose and menacing chant and then in shouts of "Long live" and "Down with." I saw arms waving the banners, I saw the pictures and the posters. I saw closed hands point at us in the Communist salute and menacingly wave the little red book of the sayings of Mao. Above all I saw faces: hostile eyes, expressions creased and hardened in hatred, wide-open mouths displaying teeth, and neck veins bulging with the effort of shouting. I saw all this. Yet, strange to say, I did not feel the sense of intimidation and apprehension which violence arouses. Everything was violent but at the same time everything was curiously lacking in violence.

What does this mean? I shouldn't like to be misunderstood. The crowd of demonstrators was certainly sincere. They were not feigning hatred. I am well aware that the fanaticism of the Red Guards is not theatrical; it is not false. But I also know that the Chinese have another side to their nature, one of unconscious and ancient culture that automatically transforms every passionate manifestation into something nervous, voluntary, and, above all, mental. As I watched the demonstrators lined up in front of the train under the station roof, the thought came to me that they could have been more violent, they could even have turned to vandalism and murder, to destruction. But this would have taken place in a manner that would be—how should I say?— entirely the work of the mind, with refined cruelty probably but without real fury. It's hard to explain what I felt. I would say that where behavior beyond the limits of perfect self-control is concerned, the Chinese always act in bad faith. But it is a kind of physiological bad faith that has nothing to do with the soul and its passions, which do not enter into it, for they have long since been trained and dominated. But the mind is sincere and its participation is sincere even if it is cold. The Chinese mind, in a cold blaze of fanatic thought, wants to be violent, and it succeeds. And there was the result, before our eyes: a political demonstration that was both fanatical and strangely lacking in true passion.

In China even the simplest and least educated peasant seems to have been born equipped with a second, "cultural" nature. In other words, culture in China is so old that it has become second nature. Even in moments of the greatest violence, private or public, the Chinese fail to reach the primitive violence of their original nature beneath the second nature they have acquired through culture. In the West, on the other hand, culture is much more recent, nothing more than a veil thrown over a primordial violence that is always ready to explode. Thus, whereas the Westerner never finds it very difficult to regress in an instant to Neanderthal man (as we saw during World War II), the Chinese, despite his efforts, remains the man of the T'ang dynasty. A curious consequence follows from this: Western man is born violent and dedicates his whole life to learning to be cultivated and civil. The Chinese, on the other hand, is born cultivated and civil and must learn to be violent. This is the explanation of the spontaneous, muscular, sanguinary, and brutal character of Western man's violence; and of the willed, nervous, mental, hysterical character of Chinese violence.

One of Confucius's sayings goes something like this: "If you take ignorant people to war, you are taking them to disaster." Granted that by ignorant people Confucius simply meant untrained people. It is still significant that even there it is instruction that is involved, not feeling. Let's skip over several centuries and come to Mao Tse-tung. As we know, Mao has been, in addition to other things, chiefly a military leader, both during the civil war against the Kuomintang nationalists and in the struggle against the Japanese invaders. The little red book of the sayings of Mao consists largely of maxims of conduct in war, and it was originally intended for the army, before it became the breviary of the Chinese people. Now it is in Mao's book that the following, undoubtedly Marxist maxim appears: "There is a gap between the ordinary civilian and the soldier, but it is no Great Wall, and it can be quickly closed, and the way to close it is to take part in revolution, in war. By saying that it is not easy to learn and to apply, we mean that it is hard to learn thoroughly and to apply skillfully. By saying that civilians can very quickly become soldiers, we mean that it is not difficult to cross the threshold. To put the two statements together, we may cite the Chinese adage, 'Nothing in the world is difficult for one who sets his mind to it.' To cross the threshold is not difficult, and mastery, too, is possible, provided one sets one's mind to the task and is good at learning."

The quotation from Mao is long; the one from Confucius is very brief. But the meaning is the same: violence is taught and learned. Man is not born violent; man is born cultivated and civil. That is, he is not born a military man but a man of letters. But we know that in the West man is born violent, without wisdom, drenched in blood and sex, primitive: for centuries Christianity has done nothing but remind us of this fact. And without indulging in considerations of a religious order, I will simply mention that in the past the Chinese child was initiated very early into the rites of respect toward his superiors (parents, teachers, leaders, emperor) and in the maxims of Confucian wisdom.

which, of course, lay at the root of those rites. The Western child, however, played—and still does—at soldiers. And only later does he turn to books—and then almost always unwillingly.

Moreover, we can compare the maxims of Confucius and Mao on training in the art of war with those of a classical Western scholar on the same subject, Clausewitz. Here is one of his thoughts: "The intervention of lucid thought or the general supremacy of mind deprives the emotional forces of a great part of their power." And another: Boldness is "virtually a creative power. . . . Happy the Army in which an untimely boldness frequently manifests itself: it is an exuberant growth which shows a rich soil. Even foolhardiness, that is boldness without an object, is not to be despised; in point of fact it is the same energy of feeling, only exercised as a kind of passion without any cooperation of the intelligent faculties."

Whereas the two Chinese, Mao and Confucius, think the civilian must learn violence, which can be taught like any other subject, the Westerner, Clausewitz, advises against removing, through instruction—that is, through the use of the intelligent faculties—the drive of the soldier's emotional force. This soldier is born violent and it is good that his violence remain intact, without mental additions or modifications. At most one should direct it toward its proper end, toward homicide, by means of severe and indecipherable discipline.

Let us turn now to the other aspect of the Chinese crowd: its impassivity. The Red Guards paraded along

the streets of Peking with their banners, their pictures
of Mao, their flutes and drums, their chants, their shouts,
waving their red books menacingly. Other Red Guards,
on a street in Canton, leaned a ladder against the wall
of a building already covered with posters, climbed up
the ladder armed with brushes and jars of paste, and
with a few energetic strokes stuck on the wall their
latest poster newspapers, the ink still damp. I was not
looking at the demonstrations then (I had not seen
many), or at the poster newspapers (they were written
in Chinese, and I don't read Chinese). I looked at the
people who were watching the demonstrations or who
had stopped, in little groups, to read the posters. And
I was invariably struck by the great number of people
who stood there impassively. Not in the impassive manner of Westerners in the face of something that arouses
displeasure or hostility, which, out of fear or calculation
or some other extrinsic motivation, they try to conceal.
No, the impassivity of the Chinese is a true impassivity, not merely apparent but profound. It is a genuine
apathy, an absolute absence of feeling. These people
were impassive because they were in fact "not there."
Of course they were physically present, in flesh and
blood, but in every other way they were somewhere
else. Where? Not, I think, in some "ideal" political or
social reality but interiorly, in a remote and deep empti-
ness. Here too I felt that I must look, as I did with violence, for a cultural explanation. These impassive
Chinese were not hostile to the parades and the posters.
They were simply letting their second nature, their

ancient cultural origin, come to the surface. Without realizing it, they had turned to Taoism, which, in the oldest Chinese tradition, constituted the obverse and complementary face of Confucianism.

Obviously, Confucianism is not violent. But it is humanistic. It believes in reason and therefore cannot but believe in that form of violence which is altogether mental and consists in the coherent application of reason. Enlightened and educational, disdainful and diffident toward anything irrational, Confucianism naturally has no difficulty being transformed into Maoism. In fact, there is no very great difference between the civil being presented in the maxims of Confucius and the proletarian rendered political that appears in those of Mao. In both, the individual is subordinate to society and simply does not exist in a private sense. In both, he must be humble and respectful toward his superiors. In both, he must consider himself eternally a student ever disposed and ready to learn. The inner man, irrational and in direct communication with the supernatural, is not mentioned by either.

Lao Tzu, however, has a great deal to say about him in the *Tao Te Ching:* "The way is empty, yet use will not drain it. Deep." And later: "In the pursuit of learning one knows more every day; in the pursuit of the way one does less every day. One does less and less until one does nothing at all, and when one does nothing at all there is nothing that is undone. It is always through not meddling that the empire is won. Should you meddle, then you are not equal to the task of win-

ning the empire." And again: "One who knows does not
speak; one who speaks does not know. Block the open-
ings; Shut the doors. Blunt the sharpness; Untangle
the knots; Soften the glare; Let your wheels move only
along old ruts. This is known as mysterious sameness."
And finally: "A man is supple and weak when living,
but hard and stiff when dead. Grass and trees are
pliant and fragile when living, but dried and shrivelled
when dead. Thus the hard and the strong are the com-
rades of death; the supple and the weak are the com-
rades of life. Therefore a weapon that is strong will not
vanquish; A tree that is strong will suffer the axe. The
strong and big takes the lower position, The supple and
weak takes the higher position."

One could go on. But these are well-known maxims,
however mysterious, and their cryptically ambiguous
and ironic meaning certainly cannot be reduced to a
psychological measure. Tao really is, as the first maxim
I quoted indicates, inexhaustible and deep. Looking
at it, however, for the convenience of my discourse,
as one of the two principal "ways" of traditional Chinese
culture (the other being the Confucian way), I think I
can hazard the hypothesis that the impassivity of so
many Chinese in the face of the Cultural Revolution
(so different from Western impassivity in similar circumstances) can be traced, albeit through the unconscious repetition of ancestral behavior, to the mystic
quietism of Tao. Thus we are faced with the disconcerting idea (disconcerting, that is, for any worldly power)
that man can withdraw inside an unplumbable inner

void. And since force is nothing but weakness, the more efficient a state or political party is, the larger and better organized it is, the weaker it is. It is the reverse for the individual who has withdrawn and entrenched himself in his own inner void. The more disarmed he seems, the more alone and weak, the stronger he really is. Of course—I repeat this—the Chinese who remain impassive in the face of the most violent manifestations of the Cultural Revolution are not all conscious Taoists. I have already said that culture in China is almost second nature. This does not alter the fact that in the West, when one speaks of Maoists and anti-Maoists, one makes the mistake of reasoning in Western fashion about matters that are not Western at all.

In my opinion, if one looks closely, one finds neither Maoists nor anti-Maoists on a public, political, and social level. Mao is stronger than ever. The Cultural Revolution has confirmed his strength, if there was any need for that. The so-called Maoists and anti-Maoists one reads about in Western newspapers are in fact the two rival, discordant branches of the same fundamental orthodoxy, which, according to the oldest and most deeply rooted Chinese tradition, I would call the orthodoxy of virtue. It is clear that this is no longer Confucian virtue, which survived for tens of centuries, but Maoist virtue, whose installation is only some twenty years old. This virtue, in the minds of the Chinese, has already taken the place of Confucian virtue, not only because of its normative and stabilizing qualities but also because of its proclaimed and evident capacity for survival. Now, at the root of Maoist virtue, as at the base of Confucian virtue, is the idea of shame and, as it is commonly called, the idea of "loss of face." Western man knows Christian sin, or shame (and repentance) in relation to himself. But a Chinese, who is primarily a social being, does not know sin. In its place is a man's shame—that is, shame (with its concomitant fear of being humiliated or of losing face) in relation to others; namely, to the society in which he lives.

Chinese "virtue," be it Confucian or Maoist, is always civic, political, social; it is totally ignorant of the inner quality of sin, of interior liberation from sin, of inner resurrection from sin. It is behavioral, based on relationships to others, who expect a certain bearing from us that we must maintain or pretend to maintain at all costs if we do not want to be humiliated or to lose face. It is evident that Maoist Communism, like Confucianism before it, can only be founded on a similar relationship between the individual and society. Thus, being a Maoist incorporates—in addition to acceptance, zeal, and fanaticism—the terror of shame, of losing face—not in a Confucian but in a Communist sense.

If one looks at Chinese affairs from the point of view of Maoist "virtue" and the fanaticism inspired by the terror of shame, I think one can assert that the only true anti-Maoists are those very Chinese who remain impassive, apathetic, indifferent in the face of the Cultural Revolution. Impassive, apathetic, indifferent, and, perhaps, unaware of being so. But in any case followers, conscious or not, of a "virtue" different from Confucian-

Maoist virtue. Apropos of this "virtue," the Book of Tao says: "I take no action and the people are transformed of themselves; I prefer stillness and the people are rectified of themselves; I am not meddlesome and the people prosper of themselves; I am free from desire and the people of themselves become simple like the uncarved block." Thus, one can see that the "virtue" which may be hidden behind impassivity, apathy, and indifference is not purely individual but, at a remove, social as well. It is a social virtue based not on zeal and propaganda, as the social virtue of the Red Guards is, but on an ineffable example—enigmatic, immobile, silent, arcane, invisible to most eyes. Elsewhere in the book of Tao we find this simple but eloquent statement: "This is called the mysterious Virtue." Here a name is supplied not for anti-Maoism but for something different from Maoism which tomorrow might become its antithesis, as Tao for centuries was the antithesis of Confucianism.

It would be risky to suggest that the impassivity of some Chinese conceals differences or even hostilities. And potential opponents, whether conscious or unconscious, are not easily identifiable. Of course: Chinese impassivity, apathy, and indifference are mixed in with and indistinguishable from the self-control that (an ancient and uninterrupted tradition) every man is expected to exercise. Thus in the end everything is uncertain, ambiguous, mysterious. Yet I believe that the Cultural Revolution, rather than facing impassivity head on, will probably end by accepting it and incor-

porating it into the Maoist system. It is that bit of indi-
vidualism, innocuous in any case, that no society, even
the most totalitarian, can afford to do without. Besides,
the Taoist Void is just as ancient and Chinese as Confucian Fullness. In the operation of revitalizing traditional China that is being carried out by Maoism, the
Void will in the end find a place for itself precisely
because it is Chinese. After all, revolution does not
mean just agitation; it also means return in a cyclical
and immutable sense. One must not forget that Mao
himself, in the book of quotations, is closer to Lao-tse
than to Marx when he says that "the law of the unity
of opposites is the fundamental law of the universe." In
fact the *Tao Te Ching* says: "The whole world recognizes
the beautiful as the beautiful, yet this is only the ugly; the
whole world recognizes the good as the good, yet this
is only the bad. Thus Something and Nothing produce
each other; The difficult and the easy complement each
other; The long and the short off-set each other; The
high and the low incline towards each other; Note and
sound harmonize with each other; Before and after
follow each other."

But Tao will always be Tao, something irreducible,
at least in the sense of Maoism. A final quotation:
"When the way was lost there was . . . benevolence . . .
rectitude . . . foreknowledge . . . and the beginning of
folly."

LOBSTER LAND

Our program for the day was the Great Wall. It runs along the mountains between China and Mongolia for more than twelve hundred miles. We visited a section about fifty miles from Peking and only saw a few hundred yards of it.

We went by automobile, sitting in our usual places: Dacia and I in back, and the driver and Mr. Li, our guide, in front. The car left Peking and headed into the country, toward the Western Hills.

It was a magnificent day. Large white clouds, gold around their edges, lazily crossed the sky. The plain of Peking was of a springtime green, bright and clear, as far as the dark blue of the hills.

The Great Wall stimulates thought. It is one of mankind's myths and not just because of its astonishing length. There is an ideology of the Great Wall—there is a message. There is also a psychology of the Great Wall, or, if you prefer, a state of mind. And finally there is a lesson in the Great Wall—aesthetic, political, military, social, philosophical, economic . . .

The Great Wall is the Chinese myth par excellence: an idea that has been transformed into a concrete object, visible, enduring, perhaps eternal. In a moment of Chinese-style conservatism, the French tried to construct their own Great Wall, the Maginot Line. But the Maginot Line did not last more than a generation; it was stormed from the flank. Now the fortresses of the Maginot Line are auctioned off to amateurs of military ruins. The Great Wall functioned uninterruptedly from 200 B.C. almost till yesterday. And the Chinese have no intention of dismantling it. They have restored the sections near Peking, and it has become the object of tourist pilgrimages. Other countries have their churches, palaces, and museums, or their Niagara Falls or Vesuviuses to show. China has a wall.

So much has been said about the Great Wall that one is almost embarrassed to mention it. One is tempted to say only the one thing that probably has not been said already—the tautology that the Great Wall is the Great Wall. But, then, the fear of uttering the commonplace is very common. So I too will have a go at the myth of the Great Wall. Let me begin by saying that the Great

Wall, obviously, has two sides to it: the inner side facing China, and the outer side facing Mongolia.

On the Chinese side there is China, an immense country that, depending on the times, either teemed with activity, prosperity, and fervor or was depopulated and ran wild in civil wars. Thus, one's idea of the Great Wall is noticeably modified. The Great Wall was not always and invariably like a strong safe protecting a treasure. Sometimes there was a treasure and sometimes not. The Great Wall actually served to protect, in a purely existential sense, the Chinese people. But from what? For that question we must consider the outer side of the Great Wall.

The Great Wall was built to prevent barbarian invasions. But who were the barbarians? One might say the Mongols, the Huns. But that would not be quite right. The barbarians were anyone not Chinese.

Yet, insofar as the Chinese were concerned, there were no other people, there could not be, not even barbarians. There was simply the void, a void created by the Great Wall itself, by the Chinese, from the moment they began to build the wall. Without the Great Wall, there could be no void.

Thus, we come closer to a true definition: the Great Wall defended and protected China from the void, from the nothing. China was what was, what existed, what was important. Outside China there was nothing, nothing existed, nothing had any importance.

The message of the Great Wall, and its ideology, then, are strictly Chinese. They are the message and the psychology of a rather special conservatism. It is not political, not military, not social, and not economic, though there is something of all this in it. One might almost say it was biological and aesthetic. The Great Wall was built to ward off the barbarians because the barbarians might introduce new blood and new ideas into China. New blood and new ideas unleash evolution and revolution—and China's aim was not to develop or change but to endure: perhaps to age, perhaps to grow decrepit, but to endure. But biological duration demands orthodoxy, immobility, etiquette, ceremony, and ritual. The Great Wall guaranteed the unending continuity of these things. It enabled the Chinese people to endure, with or without culture, in order and tranquillity or in the chaos of civil war, rich or poor. This is the biologic side of it.

There was also an aesthetic side. Every conservatism results from carrying to its extreme the idea of form as a victory over time. Only perfect form can put the object that reproduces it outside time; only through perfect form can it be expressed for eternity. Artists are conservatives par excellence, even when they claim to be revolutionaries. They want their work to endure forever.

In an artistic sense, the Great Wall was intended to maintain China unchanged for eternity. The wall had the same function as the shells of crustaceans—which would have no form were it not for the shell. One could extend the metaphor. Like crustaceans, ancient China was hard outside and soft inside, whereas men, and vertebrates in general, are soft outside and hard inside. Isn't the crustacean, then, the best symbol for a conservatism so rigid, so encrusted with laws, norms, etiquettes, ceremonies, and rites lacking in content, rites that are merely shells for soft interests? Conservatism is a lobster. Ancient China was a lobster. The Great Wall was the expression of Chinese conservatism, just as the shell, if one looks closely, is the expression of the lobster's exquisite softness.

Perhaps the barbarians were not so barbaric as the Chinese pretended they were. Or they may have been barbarians indeed, but on the order of those who invaded the Roman Empire at the time of its decline. They were bearers of the particular destruction that comes from ignorance and youth. And it was because they were young and ignorant that they brought about new developments and brought in new blood. It might perhaps have been better if the Chinese had been as thoughtless or incapable or as irresponsible as the Romans, if they had not built their Great Wall, if they had let the barbarians enter freely. They would have risked invasion, destruction, darkness. All that Europe had in the way of a Great Wall at the time of the barbarian invasions was a small Roman revetment between England and Scotland: the barbarians reached everywhere. But the Chinese, with their Great Wall, managed to keep them out for a very long time. And when the barbarians finally came, civilized by now, it was an easy matter to make them Chinese, to make them part of Chinese corruption and decrepitude. The Great Wall,

as I said, was the Chinese view of the world, their way
of existing in the world. Since they could not build a
wall on the sea, they did the next best thing and closed
their ports to the barbarians of the Western world. This
was a great wall too, and it lasted as long as the Great
Wall of stone. Then suddenly, in less than a century, all
the great walls of China fell, one after another. The
void was revealed as a difference, and China discovered
that *it* was void. China therefore has absorbed into its
inner void the outer, barbarian difference. This is the
history of modern China from the Taiping Rebellion
to Mao. Yet Chinese Communism today may face the
same problem the ancient celestial empire faced. Will
China go back to the system of the Great Wall, the biological and formal immobility guaranteed by an ideological orthodoxy, a philosophical dogma? Will it become a "lobster" land again? Or will it give up the
Great Wall once and for all? Will dogmas and ortho-
doxies be hurled down, will China become a vertebrate
land, hard inside and soft outside, a horse land (or a
man land)?

These were my thoughts as the automobile drove
through the well-cultivated countryside at the foot of
the Western Hills. Then the road began to climb. There
are magnificent mountains in China, in Sinkiang and
Tibet, under the Himalayas. But the Western Hills are
only hills. Here the Great Wall seems to be justified by
a lack of natural defenses.

The road runs along the bottom of a narrow valley,
green and flourishing. The stony river bed with shallow

limpid water is visible through the bushes. Then the hills gradually close, and though they do not grow higher, they become steeper. And the valley becomes a gorge.

We arrived at a small grouping of peasant houses, low yellow dwellings with dried-mud walls and straw roofs. The car stopped and we saw a kind of arch or bridge of white marble, a massive and elaborate structure, a veritable work of art erected there in the middle of the unchanging countryside. It was one of the gates of the Great Wall. Soldiers and excise officers probably stood guard there once. It must have been a sort of inner gate, part of a system of lesser walls that defended the nearby capital. The real Great Wall is much farther away.

We got out of the car and looked at the gate. Like all Chinese monuments, it was both massive and ornamental: solidity curiously blended with refinement. The gate was covered with fine low-relief sculptures on both sides. The subject was exactly what one would have expected, given the place and function of the monument: civilization, represented by heroes, sages, and emperors, bending the neck of barbarism, depicted in the form of dragons, serpents, and monsters. Anyone entering China would have understood at once. He was leaving the void of barbarism and entering the realm of civilization—albeit a realm consisting only of ceremony and etiquette, in fact a void like any other.

We climbed to the top of the gate. It had been abandoned, as so many artistic creations have been in China today. Weeds grew between the bricks and in the cracks in the marble; and the sculptures were scratched, darkened, defaced. It ought to be restored, but there is little chance that it can be in the near future. Mr. Li's dry and slightly bored tone as he explained the gate to us made him hesitant. The Chinese today are not interested in the Great Wall, for it no longer serves a purpose. Other times, other Great Walls. The most one can hope for is the restoration of some section of the fortifications as a military undertaking. The purpose of such a restoration would be, in accordance with the times, educational and scientific. But the marble arch is too beautiful to be restored.

We returned to the automobile and drove on through the valley, or rather the gorge. Finally, at the point where the gorge is narrowest, we saw the Great Wall, the real one, the one that traverses more than twelve hundred miles of mountains. I recognized the presence, the efficacy, the power of the myth in the emotion that suddenly took hold of me. It is true that the site is itself indescribably evocative. On both sides of the gorge the mountains seem to withdraw, as if fleeing from the gorge from one peak to another. And along the edge of these two continuous ridges that stand out against the blue sky, the huge gray stone serpent, sinuous and soft, embracing the tortuous turns of the mountain range, also takes flight. The beauty of the Great Wall lies in its faithful pursuit of the meandering mountains. A squared-up wall in the middle of a plain, such as the Escorial, for example, has something dismal, abstract, and lifeless about it. But, looking at the Great Wall, one experiences a serpentine vitality. The reptile may be decrepit but it is alive. One is almost surprised that it does not move, slithering off, curl around the mountains, and disappear into the horizon. Its vitality is subtle, insinuating, resilient, sly, tenacious, parasitic, and symbiotic. There is a kind of marriage between the wall and the mountains, a bit like the union between ivy and the tree trunk around which it twines. And this marriage is also very Chinese; it is designed to endure because it is bound to nature, a natural fact, a natural situation.

We walked up to the wall. The way in which the Chinese military engineers went about constructing the Great Wall is clear. The wall winds up and down the mountains like an amusement-park roller coaster. Where the mountain forms a peak there is a guard tower, and between one peak and another, between one tower and another, the wall descends and rises again over a distance that is never too great to prevent a clear view of anything that might happen along that particular section of wall. One has a clear view of the wall from one tower to the next. Thus the barbarians were effectively held at bay. As soon as they appeared, the soldiers stationed in the towers at the ends of the threatened section of the wall would leap to the defense. And a system of signals from tower to tower could warn Peking of an imminent attack faster than any modern telegraph.

Probably the greater part of the Great Wall has been abandoned, as have been so many monuments in China. I mean that the famous 1,200-mile extent of the wall is not intact. Overrun with weeds, its battlements crumbling, its parapets fallen, and its towers mutilated, the Great Wall must be merely a shapeless ruin of stone and brick in many places. But in that gorge near Peking the Great Wall has been restored with the greatest care. There is even a restaurant. In the open area in front of the restaurant, several tourist buses and many cars were parked. Dense groups of Chinese tourists were climbing up the wall toward the towers. They climbed slowly, looking as small as ants in the distance. They carried picnic lunches and bottles of beer wrapped in kerchiefs. The Great Wall seemed to move them and delight them more than any other monument in Peking. It is "their" monument, the only Chinese monument that has something universal to say—a myth of all mankind.

We picked out what seemed the shortest and least steep section of the wall and started to climb up too. One can go up the wall by broad steps or by extremely steep inclines. These ramps are so steep that one must crawl up them, and to come down, one must lean far back. It was a calm clear day, but there was a wild cold wind blowing at the top of the wall—evidently the wind that whirls in the void beyond the wall. And there was the void: we looked out between the battlements at it. Beyond the gorge, past a kind of ridge of shrubs, was an immense green plain, bright, golden in the sun, mysterious and thriving. And the thought came back of the void from which the wall was to protect China. It was just something different and perhaps—who knows —something better. Perhaps the Great Wall was meant not only to defend and protect but to prevent comparisons and confrontations.

Be that as it may, the revolution that has renovated China came from there, from that immense plain, mysterious, green, and golden in the sun. Over there, in a straight line running thousands of miles, is Lenin's Russia and Marx's Europe. Over there is the homeland of the barbarian ideas that have rejuvenated the decrepit old lady with her tiny feet and age-old etiquette. The danger now is that these barbarian ideas will be bound up, like ladies' feet, in orthodox dogma, that they too will become matters of etiquette, ceremony, and ritual.

We walked up several steps and then began to clamber up a tremendously steep ramp. We climbed into the wind, which struck from all sides and seemed to want to hurl us down. We finally reached a guard tower. It was three stories high, with rooms and stairs and passageways. There were crenels for shooting arrows and projectiles, and small windows for the mouths of culverins. Everything had been marvelously restored. Everything was brand-new and dead.

I turned to our guide. "I suppose the Great Wall at least served some purpose."

"It protected the empire for centuries from barbarian invasion."

"But what happened in China during all those centuries?"

"Well, it's clear what happened. First the empire grew and prospered, and then it went into decline."

"So the Great Wall at some point no longer managed to protect China from its own decadence and corruption."

He shrugged his shoulders, and deep down I knew he was not wrong to do so. My remark was a sophism. "There is no relation between the two. On the one hand, the empire built the Great Wall for purely military reasons. And on the other, China went into decline."

"Let's have a closer look at this. Try to understand me. If China had not built the Great Wall and had remained open to foreign influences and ideas and innovations, perhaps it would not have gone into decline."

"There was no chance of beneficial ideas or influences or innovations coming from Mongolia. Just armed warriors on horseback."

"I haven't made myself clear. For me the Great Wall is chiefly a symbol."

"A symbol of what?"

"The symbol of invincible Chinese conservatism."

"Nothing's invincible. China today is a revolutionary country, the most revolutionary country in the world. And the Great Wall is a great work of Chinese military engineering."

When our visit was ended and we returned to the car that was to take us back to Peking, I couldn't resist quoting Lao Tzu's words of the Tao.

"The court is corrupt,
The fields are overgrown with weeds,
The granaries are empty;
Yet there are those dressed in fineries,
With swords at their sides,
Filled with food and drink,
And possessed of too much wealth.
This is known as taking the lead in robbery.
Far indeed is this from the way."

These words were written before the Great Wall was built. What can Great Walls protect except that which should not be protected? Life, at its fullest and most mature, has no need of Great Walls.

HATE FOR THE PAST

Our guide, Mr. Li, was a thin yellow man. (Not all Chinese are yellow; on the contrary, very few of them are.) His expression was one of decrepit sadness. He had a nervous tic that made one half of his face jump up and down while the other half remained motionless. And he stuttered. Mr. Li was sad and neurotic. And when he laughed it was a sardonic, acid, bitter little laugh. His sadness was silent and meditative, like that of someone who had resigned himself to something inevitable and unpleasant. If I hadn't known that guides are chosen among people of unblemished political fidelity, I would have thought that Mr. Li was not a convinced Maoist. But that wasn't the case. Mr. Li was sad because he was sad. And he did not even realize that he was sad.

The weather had changed, as it often does in Peking. The sun had been shining the day before; now it was drizzling. A gray cloud had come from the Western Hills and was oozing thin trickles of rain, like water poured from a child's watering can. The roads glimmered, and the usual parades of the Cultural Revolution had turned into processions of long-hooded raincoats that reminded one of religious orders. Mao's religion found full confirmation in the rain: like the pictures, standards, and columns of the brothers of the Bona Mors.

As soon as we were in the automobile, Mr. Li said, "Today we're going to the Summer Palace."

"In the rain?" I asked.

"In the rain."

The car drove on. Mr. Li was not talkative, but he was attentive. We were passing a building covered, almost plated, in poster newspapers, and Dacia had picked up her camera to take a picture. With a gesture that was sober, sad, and discreet at the same time, Mr. Li, who had seemed to be deep in conversation with the driver, reached back and put his hand on her shoulder to ask her not to. One cannot photograph poster newspapers; it is forbidden. The poster newspapers often contain—along with insults and invective, "long-lives" and "down-withs"—some objective truths, truths yet to be achieved, sometimes proclaiming events that are to take place months later. All this is for local consumption. Foreigners have no business poking in their noses. But I am still not sure whether Mr. Li's gesture was motivated by Maoist zeal or whether he wanted to show the driver that he knew his duty. Perhaps both, given the well-known mutual surveillance to which the Chinese submit each other.

The car drove on through the streets of Peking. At one point I said to Mr. Li, "War broke out last night between Israel and the Arab states."

"Really? How did you find out about it?"

"From some Swedish students who had heard it from the Swedish ambassador, who heard it on the radio."

Mr. Li said nothing. His wrinkled face, throbbing with a variety of tics, betrayed no curiosity whatsoever.

"You Chinese haven't the slightest interest in the outside world, in what is happening in the outside world," I said.

"Why do you say that? Didn't you see the demonstrations of the Red Guards outside the English and Syrian embassies?"

"I'm not talking about demonstrations. I'm talking about interest, about curiosity. Throughout this trip I have asked the Chinese people you've introduced me to hundreds of questions about China. But no one has ever asked me anything about Europe."

Mr. Li looked at me in silence.

I waited a moment and then went on. "I'm not saying it is something negative or positive; I'm just saying it's characteristic of the Chinese. In Europe we have private collections and public museums full of works of Chinese art. Not to mention the studies Englishmen, Frenchmen, Germans, and Americans have written on Chinese art and history and culture. But there is nothing comparable in China. I was in Shanghai before the war, in 1936. There were some very rich people, some of the richest in the world, there. But no one collected European painting, sculpture, drawings, ceramics, precious objects, or works of art. There simply was no interest in Europe."

Mr. Li turned to me and said, "They were capitalists."

"European collectors are capitalists too."

Mr. Li said nothing. I ended up saying, "The motive may be this: China has always considered itself the center of the world. It gave but it didn't receive. Nor did it want to receive."

We had reached the open area in front of the entrance to the Summer Palace. The magnificent bronze lions and dragons that guard the entrances were swarming with Red Guards, who were having their pictures taken perched on those masterpieces of traditional Chinese art. We went inside, and soon after, something fantastic happened. Somebody hurried past me. It was an elderly Chinese gentleman dressed in extreme, incredible elegance—the first and only such figure I saw during my entire stay in China. He wore a panama hat, an ivory-colored raw-silk tunic and trousers; the fabric was heavy and clearly of excellent quality, and of perfect cut. He carried a jade-topped malacca walking stick. His face was cold, scornful, and impassive and was trimmed by a traditional short white beard. He went past me and disappeared. I scarcely believed my eyes. I had no wish to ask my guide about him, knowing full well that he would reply ambiguously and evasively or simply deny having seen the man. I preferred to let my imagination run wild. A former mandarin? A former industrialist left to run his own factory? Or—and this idea was the most absurd, which may be why I liked it best—the former emperor of China, the last one, who would have been about seventy, like the old gentleman in the raw-silk suit. They say that he was a librarian and that he wrote a book of memoirs: *The Last Manchu.*

We went for a walk around the lake of the Summer Palace. There were several pavilions and other places of delight on the banks of this artificial lake and hidden among the hills overlooking it. The order of our stroll was this. Mr. Li walked ahead of us at some distance. Then came the two of us, then a group of people who stared at us open-mouthed and adjusted their pace to ours. Every now and then Mr. Li would turn around and cast an inscrutable glance at us, something between the protective and the bored. The people then would realize that we weren't alone and on our own, that we too were dependent on the authority of the Chinese state—and that seemed to reassure them. But they continued to follow us and stare at us.

Since it was still drizzling, we walked under a kind of open gallery that ran along the lake a short distance from its shore. It must have sheltered the emperor and his court from sun and rain as they went to the various pavilions of delight scattered around the lake. It was all wood. The pillars and railings and ceilings were covered with paintings. For the most part the decorations were traditional motifs. But at every pair of pillars there was an oval on the architrave with genre scenes and landscapes. The landscapes had the delicacy and precision of etchings. And their very precision suggested a very Chinese kind of surrealism. The subject was always the same: a building (a tower, house, villa, pavilion, portico, balcony, or look-out), always in a different position, against a natural or artificial background (park, garden, country road, hedge) or wilderness. These landscapes had three elements: brickwork, vegetation, and water (canals, rivers, lakes, pools, etc.). A single subject, as I said, but it is incredible how many variations the unknown artists, or craftsmen, who painted these ovals managed to create. I spoke of surrealism, but this was an involuntary surrealism of the ancients, unconsciously dreamlike, enchanted and enchanting.

The oval genre scenes, the scenes in which human figures appear, were, however, all covered with a coat of pink, the bright false pink of certain toothpastes. The pink was transparent, thinned perhaps by the rain and the sun, and one could see small figures, surely no less enchanting than the landscapes. I turned to Mr. Li. "Why have these scenes been covered with a coat of pink paint?"

He replied calmly with the dutiful lie. "They haven't been restored yet."

It wasn't true. And he knew that I knew that he knew it wasn't. The genre scenes have in fact been painted over because they depict the powerful men of the past absorbed in a tranquil, innocent, happy, gracious, pleasant, and refined life. And the people must not learn anything of the past, or at least of this aspect of the past. The past consisted only of landowners who martyred the peasants. Now, it is true that most of the landowners behaved inhumanly to their serfs. But it had never occurred to Mr. Li and to those concerned with propaganda in China that those very landowners, cruel and odious as they were, were at the same time men of refinement, well-bred, versed in letters, disciples of Confucius, sensitive to beauty, and immersed in the activities depicted in the ovals now painted over in pink. This sort of contradiction is not acknowledged by the propaganda. Yet the little red book of the sayings of Mao insists on almost every page that reality consists of contradictions, that without contradictions there can be no reality.

We spent a long time in the gallery with two goggle-eyed groups, one to the right and one to the left, which followed us at a distance under the rain. We looked at the paintings. Mr. Li, as sad as could be, preceded us with his hands clasped behind his back.

We stopped to look at the famous marble ship anchored forever in the gray water of the Summer Palace lake. It is said that the Chinese parliament had authorized funds to create a navy comparable to Western navies. But the empress appropriated the funds to adorn the Summer Palace, and among other things, with un-conscious (or perhaps conscious) irony she had this small naval monument erected—one of those steamboats with a waterwheel and a tall slender smokestack that must have plied the Chinese rivers about the middle of the last century. I asked Mr. Li, "The marble boat is still a great attraction for the Chinese, isn't it?"

"Yes. Do you see how many people there are?"

The boat was indeed full of people, boys and girls and babies, women and old people going up and down the stairs, laughing and shoving. The exterior of the boat was marble, but inside it was equipped like a real boat, with mahogany woodwork, mirrors, brasses, velvet sofas, wood-paneled floors. But everything was worn out, lusterless, dirty, listless, decaying. I commented to Mr. Li: "Most of Peking's monuments are in terrible condition and they're terribly looked after. Why is that?"

"There are more urgent things to do than restore monuments."

"The Temple of Heaven, for example, where we were yesterday. Most of those beautiful violet ceramic tiles are cracked or broken. And the marvelous woods around the temple, not to mention the temple itself, are full of waste paper and refuse and filth. Why?"

"The Red Guards were bivouacked in the Temple of Heaven last winter."

"At least you could have cleaned it up."

"The Temple of Heaven can last another hundred years at least just as it is."

As he made this remark, he shrugged his shoulders with an air of indifference and boredom. Actually China is just on the threshold of that ultimate death of monuments which we call tourism. For the moment the Chinese simply "hate" their monuments. Because, and let this be clearly understood, the Chinese hate their past, be it artistic or literary, philosophic or religious. Why? It isn't easy to say. They hate it not so much because it is the past (as the Futurists, for example, hated the past) as because they consider it a mistake, a bourgeois error, a capitalist error. However, alongside this hatred for the past—the more remarkable in a country which maintained the cult of ancestors for three thousand years—China has a patriotic and xenophobic nationalism that is probably the most intense and aggressive in the world today. Everywhere else nationalism is accompanied by glorification of the past. But not in China.

In my opinion, this contradiction can be explained by the almost pathological conservatism that characterized traditional China from its origins until yesterday, a conservatism that was not so much economic, social, or religious in origin as it was—how should I say?—biological. China, that is, was concerned with enduring rather than with developing. And duration is often synonymous with repetition. China, then, was conservative in the same way that nature is conservative. One cannot scold nature for repeating the same things every year, the seasons and all the changes of the seasons. This repetition happens in all peasant societies, but rarely with the regularity, refinement, and immobility of China. A human copy of nature, China repeated nature's serenity, monotony, permanence, impassivity, and fatality. China was conservative, and it became reactionary only when the empire was corrupted and then attacked and blackmailed by foreigners on all sides.

I believe the Cultural Revolution is aimed chiefly at restoring a "natural" conservatism in China, a conservatism suited to modern times and capable of enduring for thousands of years like that of the empire. The Chinese hatred for the past, then, is the hatred of an emerging conservatism (in the end, all revolutions are conservative, for they must preserve the conquests of the revolution) for a dying conservatism. The former is taking the place of the latter. But since the latter is slow in dying, it must be hatred.

This is the goal of any kind of conservatism in China: not so much to protect interests as to assure by any means the continuity, rather the eternity, of the Chinese people. It is not a question of merely material continuity or eternity, but of continuity based on a fundamental harmony with reality (one used to say "harmony with heaven"). And this harmony is achieved by any orthodoxy that can provide immobility and, in a certain sense, place China outside history, at least for a few centuries. In fact, what one usually speaks of as the history of China, at least until now, has been a series of distinct periods marked by the name of a dynasty during which history itself was virtually suspended. Then the last dynasty ended in corruption and military disaster. And the Chinese social system collapsed into anarchy, until, by means of catastrophic upheaval, a new orthodoxy was established, a new harmony with reality or with heaven and, consequently, a new immobility outside history. It follows that in China history is disorder, anguish, anarchy, hunger, and war. Whereas peace, prosperity, civilization, and culture stand for the absence of history. Nowadays the Chinese hate their past because this hate is useful for the purposes of that future orthodoxy which will be built exclusively of Maoist materials. In my opinion, this is the explanation of the vandalism of the Red Guards, who are ruining the monuments, burning the books, and furiously destroying everything that is left of old China. In any case, the Chinese consider themselves inexhaustible. The past destroyed will be replaced by a future that is equally rich in wisdom and refinement. Let me repeat that China is like nature—with every season it returns and bears its fruit.

After the Summer Palace, the day's program included a visit to the Ming tombs. It is one of the most beautiful sites in the environs of Peking. For a change, the complete neglect in which China's monuments are abandoned enhances the beauty of the place. Imagine a vast plain covered with wild shrubs, an occasional tree here and there, closed in on three sides by the low blue mounts, soft and lovely, which classical Chinese literature has immortalized in the name of Western

Hills. The wild growth on the plain is tall and thick, but if one looks closely, one can distinguish in the pullulating vegetation the occasional pavilion roofs that indicate the locations of the imperial tombs. This uncertainty and the distance and the isolation are no small part of the elegiac and melancholy beauty of the place.

One enters the plain through propylaea of white marble with violet ceramic tiles, with tall weeds growing all around. A rough irregular path is flanked by two rows of large statues of lions, chimeras, dragons, horses, elephants, camels, and warriors. The statues are slightly more or slightly less than life size. They all bear the seal of Chinese genius, the unmistakable style, or stylization, that is at once bizarre and full of good sense, rustic and refined, monumental and familiar, realistic and decorative, ritual and worldly. The statues are right up against the undergrowth, which sprouts up behind them, and they stand in the midst of weeds and the dust of the path. They do not have bases or pedestals. It is as if they had been put down temporarily until a proper and final place could be found for them. I asked Mr. Li how many Ming tombs there were.

"Thirteen."

He nodded toward the scrub. Actually, all I could make out in the endless growth of shrubs were three or four distant pavilion roofs, widely separated one from another.

"Thirteen pavilions. How many of the tombs have been evacuated so far?"

"Only one."

"How did you find it?"

"In 1956, when a wall was being repaired, a tablet was found with an exact description of the tomb, which was located behind the pavilion, under a hill. We followed the instructions on the tablet and found a round well full of humus. We removed the humus and found the door of the tomb at the bottom of the well."

"Who was buried in the tomb?"

"An emperor and two empresses."

It was drizzling and we were in a wood of tall straight pines. Between the trunks there were two small, one-story, prefabricated structures, one on the left and one on the right. These were the two small museums in which the objects found in the tomb were displayed. At the end of the wood, one could see the ancient votive pavilion at the head of a staircase. The guide went on ahead of us and walked to the back of the pavilion. Behind the pavilion was the hill. The base had been cut open in a triangular excavation, and a door could be seen at the end. That was the actual tomb of the emperor, the one described on the tablet.

We approached the door and went down a broad spiral staircase to the bottom of an enormous well, which had once been full of humus. It grew colder as we descended, a veritable sepulchral cold. The walls of the well were blotched with damp and encrusted with a greenish mold. We reached the bottom. There was a pair of white marble doors with white marble bosses, exact replicas of the red-lacquer doors with gold bosses in the imperial palaces. We entered the first room. In it was a white marble throne. (It too was probably an exact replica of a real throne of precious wood.) There were several cylindrical cushions, also of marble, and on a pedestal an enormous Ming porcelain vase, white, with the faintest blue cast, and decorated with blue patterns of dragons and flowers. We went over to the vase, lifted the lid, and saw that it was two-thirds full of a blackish liquid on which a sort of dark cream had crusted. It was votive oil several centuries old that had been left there in witness of a cult now dead (the cult of the emperor). We left the first room and passed through another marble door, similar to the first one, and entered another room. In it was another marble throne, and cylindrical marble seats, and a porcelain vase full of votive oil. A third door and another throne, with seats and vase. At the end of the hypogeum there was a large room, the coldest and barest of all, containing a number of large boxes, painted red, some square and some oblong. "These cases," Mr. Li explained, "contained the bodies of the emperor and the two empresses, as well as all the objects you'll be seeing in the museums. Actually these cases are copies of the originals, which were rotted by the dampness and putrefying with decay."

Mr. Li spoke of the emperor and the empresses with profound and genuine dislike. After a moment he added: "When an emperor died, he was buried in this way. But when a peasant died, they dug a hole next to his house, threw some dirt on him, and that was that."

We were happy to get outside again. We went to

visit the two museums. Carefully displayed in the glass cases were delicately chased jades, solid-gold plates, imperial sceptres studded with precious stones, imperial crowns shaped like cowls covered with gold pendants and gems, finely carved ivories, trinkets, necklaces, rings, and other such objects. There was also a great deal of Ming porcelain, blue and white, of beautiful workmanship.

I turned to Mr. Li. "You've made a discovery that, in archaeological importance and value, is comparable to that of the tomb of Tutankhamen in Egypt."

"This was done for scientific and educational purposes. The people must be educated."

"That's all very well, but beauty, too, can educate."

"There's nothing beautiful about it. But it is a good thing that the people know how the emperors were buried."

Was he serious? He probably was. In China today the sense of the beautiful has been replaced by the sense of the good. This tomb is not beautiful, because it is not good. But it can be educational, that yes.

"Do you think there are comparable tombs behind the other twelve pavilions?" I asked him.

"Who knows?"

"Aren't you investigating?"

"No."

"Why not?"

"This one is enough. What's the point of excavating the others? One is enough for education."

DON GIOVANNI'S
DINNER GUEST

The Cultural Revolution has set the negative seal of
bourgeois origin, that is, of evil (not merely external
and social, but internal and psychological), on everything that is individual and not politically assimilated.
Which amounts to saying that the Cultural Revolution
is puritanical. But one must not make the mistake of
thinking that Chinese puritanism is anything like
Calvinist Anglo-Saxon puritanism, although they have
the same philosophical and ideological implications.
No, Chinese puritanism is simply an extension to urban
life of rural values and usage. Here too Maoism, that
paradoxical reversal of Marxism, finds visible confirmation. The peasants wore patched clothing—jacket and

trousers. Now all urban China wears jacket and trousers and patches. The peasants never knew the pleasures of sex (pleasures which some maintain constitute the chief difference between man, who can enjoy sex, and animal, which only knows how to procreate). Now all of urban China is permeated by a peasant, antisexual prudishness. And the peasants ate badly (when they ate at all). Inspired by the peasants' sobriety, the Cultural Revolution has closed all restaurants in the cities. Even in Peking, all restaurants but one have been closed. Until a year ago, Peking restaurants served excellent food prepared according to the recipes of traditional Chinese cuisine, every bit as refined and complicated as French cuisine. Particularly popular were restaurants offering regional specialties from the near and distant provinces of this immense country. Now the Cultural Revolution has closed all these restaurants except one, near the Square of the Temple of Heavenly Peace.

Why has this one restaurant been left open? I wondered about it a number of times and found no satisfactory answer. I knew that foreign visitors were generally invited there to traditional, hence excellent, dinners. We had been informed that the restaurant was left open officially for the benefit of tourists. Peking duck was served in the same way that the Temple of Heaven was put on display. I suspected, however, that on an unconscious level, there was another reason. After much thought, I reached the following conclusion. That one restaurant had been left open for educational purposes. Those who were invited there for a meal, all of them Western visitors—hence bourgeois—should be made to realize, as they devoured the delicate dishes of ancient Chinese cuisine, that they were committing an infraction, a transgression, almost a crime. Every now and then they were spared the poor food of the mass-tourist hotels and were allowed to eat splendidly as people had in restaurants before the Cultural Revolution. But with a sense of guilt. And digestion would consequently be accompanied by regret, repentance, and persuasion. This, I repeat, may all have been done unconsciously. Perhaps consciously all that was intended was one more attraction on the tourist program. But in reality (the unconscious reality of the Cultural Revolution) a lesson was meant to be taught. It was something like what happened in Italy after the abolition of houses of prostitution. A single house was left open for educational purposes, so that people could see how foul prostitution was and therefore develop a salutary sense of guilt.

One evening toward the end of our stay in Peking, our guide said to us before leaving: "Tonight you won't be eating in the hotel."

"Why not?"

"You're going to dine in a restaurant. You will have Peking duck."

"What is Peking duck?"

"It's Peking's most famous local dish. All you will be served is duck."

"Only duck?"

"Yes, only duck. It's very good."

"Will you be joining us to eat Peking duck?"

It was a superfluous question. I don't know why, it just came out. The guide never ate with us. It was forbidden, or perhaps (as it happens in China) it was "discouraged." We were Westerners and hence bourgeois. So it was just as well that the guide not eat with us. This reminded me somewhat of India, where Europeans are left to eat by themselves, by the Brahmins because they are afraid of being sullied, and by the pariahs because they are afraid of sullying.

"How will we get to the restaurant by ourselves?" I asked.

"The driver will take you to the restaurant and wait outside until you've finished. Then he'll take you back to the hotel."

"Just the two of us?"

"Just the two of you."

He left us and we went up to our room in the hotel. There were two immense dining rooms in the hotel, one of the largest in Peking; one served Chinese food and the other served Western food. There was always a crowd in the Chinese dining room—delegations, groups, tables-full. We were the only ones in the Western dining room. The six or seven waitresses in the Western dining room had almost nothing to do. While one of them served us, the others sat on the window sills looking out on the street and the perpetual spectacle of the Cultural Revolution—demonstrations, parades, processions. There was very little difference between the food served in the Chinese-style dining room and that served in the Western one. In the Chinese dining room the food, mostly fried, was served already cut up into small pieces and was eaten with chopsticks. The same food, fried in the same way, was served in large pieces in the Western dining room, and it was eaten with a knife and fork.

Our bedroom was Russian in style, tsarist and nineteenth-century. The Cultural Revolution had not yet reached it. It was divided into two sections by an archway in the middle. On one side were two monumental beds with mattressed quilts and enormous pillows. On the other was a sofa and chairs with gray slipcovers and antimacassars on the arms and backs. There was a teapot, cups, a thermos of boiling water, and a tea bag on a small table. One might have sat down in this part of the room perhaps to read quietly. We did, in fact, have a great many Maoist pamphlets, books, and brochures. But it was impossible to read. Outside, nailed above the window, was a loudspeaker that began blaring at six in the morning and did not let up until nightfall. It blared with a voice that was sometimes soft and strained, feminine, and then again it would be serious, though no less strained, masculine. Evidently it blared the texts of Mao. Thus we were faced with a paradoxical contradiction. The texts of Mao on the loudspeaker, which we could not understand because they were shouted in Chinese, kept us from reading the texts of Mao in English and French translations that we could understand—the tricks of propaganda.

When we got to the room, Dacia and I had a brief

consultation. We were invited to dinner. How should we dress? Usually we dressed in Chinese fashion, short-sleeved shirt and trousers. But after the day's activities our shirts and trousers were soiled and wrinkled. We'd have to change. But into what?

"Put on a skirt and blouse, and I'll wear my blue suit."

"No skirt. The Chinese don't like skirts. It's a mark of bourgeois corruption. Don't you remember, they spit at me the first day?"

"That was a baby."

"Yes, but a baby that listens to the radio."

"Well then, wear trousers as usual. I'll put on my blue suit. It's all I have."

"Without a tie, though."

"Why can't I put on a tie?"

"Ties are a symbol of the bourgeoisie in China. It's no accident that one never sees ties. Everyone has a tunic buttoned to the neck or a Robespierre shirt."

We left the room about eight. The corridors were gloomy, poorly lit, and tsarist, nineteenth-century, Dostoevskian. In the vestibule of our floor the porter took our key. We got into an elevator that in any Western hotel would have been used only for freight. The filthy walls were crudely painted yellow, and the doors were iron. The young girl who ran the elevator chattered with the people that crowded in. They were all Chinese. The hotel was called the Hotel of Nations and was intended to house foreign visitors, but we were the only ones at the time. The other guests seemed to be homeless functionaries or people on official business.

I watched them as the elevator made its endless descent, stopping at every floor. They wore short-sleeved shirts or military jackets buttoned to the neck. Their clothes were clean, recently washed, but full of tiny wrinkles because they were never pressed. There was a mixed smell of disinfectant and cabbage in the air—the disinfectant used to clean the elevator and the cabbage that represents one of China's basic foods. The Chinese did not look at us at all. They were educated people and fairly sophisticated. The streets, however, were full of simple, ingenuous peasants visiting Peking from distant provinces, and everywhere they stared at us. We were followed, surrounded by people who unabashedly stared at us, their mouths open in amazement, as all peasants stare. Most of all they looked at Dacia's blue eyes. In China, I was told, blue eyes are a sign of exceptional ferocity and wickedness. Don't suppose, though, that the hatred of blue eyes is the result of recent xenophobic campaigns against the Anglo-Saxons and the Russians. The horror of blue eyes seems to date back to the Mongol invasions. The Mongols were frequently blue-eyed.

We finally reached the lobby of the hotel, a lugubrious, official, Soviet affair: a vast, dull, dark-colored floor; squat, dark, square pillars; and poor, coarse draperies, invariably dark-colored. In the middle of the lobby, against a large red-velvet screen, stood an immense, pure-white plaster statue of Mao. Around the statue and on the red-carpeted steps leading up to its pedestal there was a profusion of fresh flowers, just as there is in Catholic churches around the altar of a saint. All that was missing were candles and censers. I stopped to look at the statue. It was in the edifying and realistic Stalinist style: Mao depicted smiling, with the famous wart on his chin; dressed in the famous military tunic buttoned to the neck (all the buttons were shown), and the famous wide trousers with the low crotch that the Chinese wear. It saddened me to think that Mao, at seventy-four and after a lifetime free of adulation, should wind up, even for political reasons, by turning to the cult of personality, like Stalin before him and certainly more obsessively than Stalin himself. In Moscow there used to be plaster statues of Stalin in the hotel lobbies, just like this one of Mao. It made me sadder still that the expression was the same in the statues of Stalin and Mao—smiling, affable, paternal. Stalin had a merciless, bloodthirsty character behind that expression. Mao, who is neither merciless nor bloodthirsty, had no need to turn himself into a father of peoples. But that is the way things are. Evidently peasants throughout the world have the same tastes. The man who governs, ferocious or not, must be depicted for them as a benevolent and protective father. I looked at the statue for a long time. Considering the plaster and the armature, it must have weighed several hundred pounds. It reminded me of something or someone, but I wasn't sure. I tried to think what it was, but couldn't. And we left the hotel.

It was night and quite dark. The nineteenth-century street lamps, with clusters of globes something like those in the Place de l'Opéra in Paris, were only lighted at the top, as an economy measure. The last swarms of bicycles passed by silently in the shadows. Three boys wearing the arm bands of the Red Guards were beating furiously on an immense drum outside the hotel entrance, but the dismal thump echoed down the street without disturbing its solemn rural peace. It was almost like a country road at dusk, when the last hands head for home on their bicycles.

Our car was there, doors open, waiting for us. We got in and started down the street among the cyclists. Occasionally a truck sped past us, overflowing with workers or Red Guards with banners in the wind. And occasionally we saw the usual, religious-style processions—the picture of Mao carried by two girls, then the banners, and behind them the demonstrators in single file, each clutching his copy of the little red book of the sayings of Mao.

We reached Tien An Men Square, passed the obelisk dedicated to the history of modern China—from the Taiping Rebellion until today—went around the monumental gate with its slanting buttresses and its upturned triple roof, and headed for a crowded street of old Peking. Where the walls once stood flanking the gate, there were now pits, mounds of rubble, and scaffolding all around—construction work for a subway. We turned into a side street. Every now and then we passed a flame-red building covered with gold ideograms, headquarters of state or party organizations. Suddenly the car stopped, and we saw a double door that was almost indecently Western in appearance. Someone peered out the window and as soon as he saw us disappeared. It was the entrance to the restaurant. Embarrassed and shamefaced, we got out of the car, went through the crowd, and entered the restaurant.

Again, as in the hotel, we felt as if we had been carried back in time and transported to Europe, but it was a past time and a Europe filtered through tsarist Russia. The entrance was neoclassic, with a black-and-white checkered floor, two matching sofas covered in shabby, dusty red velvet, two large yellowed mirrors with Empire frames. A V-shaped staircase led to the upper floor, and a worn-out red carpet slithered up the white marble steps. The upper floor had been divided into several small dining areas separated by brown plastic partitions. We were taken to one of these rooms. There was a large round table under a Bohemian glass chandelier with crystal pendants and prisms that gave a very faint light. There were only two chairs, and two places set at a great distance from each other. We were to dine alone then, as if on a romantic rendezvous. The window was covered with heavy floral-patterned draperies. The window was locked, and the poster newspapers pasted on the panes prevented us from looking out. One of the many loudspeakers on the street blared incessantly, like the loudspeaker outside the window of our hotel room. I got up and looked through the cracks in the partitions at the adjacent dining areas. In the one on the right sat a man and a woman, both Chinese, surely some functionary and his wife. They ate seriously and demurely, without speaking. In the one on the left there were three Japanese and three Chinese. Perhaps a business dinner. I could sense an air of embarrassment, of mutual mistrust. I went back and sat down, and for a while we sat in silence, looking at each other. Then we both broke out laughing—some invitation! Alone, trapped in a squalidly intimate dining room, without Chinese dinner guests, with the windows sealed and the panes blocked by poster newspapers, and with a loudspeaker that kept us from hearing each other because of the blare of its incomprehensible (for us) propaganda. Alone and compelled to feel guilty for eating Peking duck in a country that lives on rice, millet, and cabbage.

At last a lovely, gracious waitress arrived with hors d'oeuvres. We had been warned that the dinner would consist exclusively of duck. And in fact the hors d'oeuvres consisted of slices of duck liver, pieces of cold roast duck, and strips of duck skin. A few minutes later we had an incredible sight before us, a veritable surrealist apparition: exactly like a French chef, complete with white apron tied at the waist and a white cap on his head, the cook looked in and, with the traditional gesture typical of Parisian restaurants, he presented a whole roast duck for our approval. He offered it for our inspection before passing it on to the carver. We nodded our approval.

Another quarter hour passed. The radio blared, we

had finished the hors d'oeuvres, and we sat looking at each other. Our waitress returned with a plate of roast duck liver. It was served with a pleasant-tasting white flour. The duck liver was exquisite.

"It's excellent," I said.

"Marvelous."

"We've never eaten so well in China."

"Yes, it's the first time we've had really good food."

"But when we eat in the hotel, even though we eat badly, we eat the same food everyone else does, and so we eat happily. Here we are eating well, but with a feeling of guilt."

"Why?"

"Because the people, the overwhelming majority of the Chinese people, do not have much chance of eating Peking duck, if they have any chance at all. And because we've been put in here alone, in this sinister capitalist private dining room, to be served a meal that during the Bell Époque would have finished with champagne and a sofa. Except that here the radio and the poster newspapers remind us that the Bell Époque is long since gone. Do you know what I think?"

"What?"

"I feel like Don Giovanni in the last act. It's as if I had dared the noble statue of the great Commendatore to join us for dinner, but in this case it's the white plaster statue of Mao in our hotel lobby. As if impiously but boldly I had invited him to dine with us on Peking duck. And in a moment you will hear the slow, heavy step—weighty, terrible—and you will hear a basso profundo: 'Don Giovanni, you have invited me to dinner, and I have come.' And then the statue will take my hand and drag me to hell. To a capitalist hell, of course."

"What statue? I don't understand what you mean."

"I told you, Mao's statue, the one in our hotel lobby."

"What has Don Giovanni got to do with Mao's China?"

"Don Giovanni is the impious and bold Westerner par excellence. All Westerners are or could be Don Giovanni."

"All right, but the Commendatore isn't Mao."

"Of course he is. Don't you remember: 'Repent, change your ways. This is your last hour'? Those could be the words of Mao to any capitalist or revisionist, in his well-known, Confucian-inspired didactic and educational manner. Don Giovanni, alas, can only reply: 'No, no, I will not repent.' Mao the Commendatore insists, 'Repent, scoundrel!' And Don Giovanni must reply, 'No, you old fool.' The conflict is irremediable. You and I are Don Giovanni. Soon Mao will arrive, or rather his statue will, its step weighing several hundred pounds of plaster."

"You always joke."

"So did Don Giovanni."

We both started laughing, but the picture was lugubrious and obstinately symbolic and significant: two bourgeois at table, with the blare of the radio and the windows covered with poster newspapers. The light was weak and sorrowful, just right for a funeral dinner.

We heard footsteps, but to tell the truth, they were very light. The door opened.

"It's Mao's statue. Get ready."

It was the waitress with a tray bearing the main course, several pieces of roast duck. We ate. The skin was crisp and fragrant, roasted outside and fatty inside. The flesh was white and delicate, very light and cooked just right. With the roast duck, the waitress served us duck broth, with dainty slices of cucumber and mushroom.

"It's too bad," Dacia remarked. "When we're at the hotel I'm always hungry and the food is terrible. Now the food is marvelous, and I'm not hungry at all."

"Pass it over. I'll eat your portion as well as my own. True, I feel guilty. But since I'm sinning, I want to sin all the way, even if I explode."

The waitress came in again, this time with breast of duck. She returned still another time, with a light and delicate broth of duck wings. We drank hot rice wine, iced beer, and jasmine tea. The loudspeakers blared louder than ever.

"So the statue didn't come after all," I remarked. "I wonder why."

"Maybe because we're already in the capitalist hell. So there was no need for him to conduct us there."

"I think that if the statue had come, he would simply have given us the little red book of the sayings of Mao and then would have gone on his way. There is no one in the Chinese hell. No one in China is really damned. With the proper brain-washing, everyone can be saved and reeducated. Redeemed, thanks to reading Mao's book, from the capitalist way and set on the way of Maoism."

"You like the idea of Mao's statue and Don Giovanni because you're a writer, and you've got to poke literature in everywhere. But this isn't a music festival at Spoleto. We're in Peking."

"No, you don't understand me. The idea that Mao's statue has a function similar to that of the Commendatore in *Don Giovanni* is simply an expression of the sense of guilt which the Chinese, intentionally or not, have made me feel this evening by inviting us to dine on duck in this restaurant. If they weren't so obsessed with this mania for education, they would have closed this one surviving establishment of bourgeois delights and exported their duck for foreign currency and bought material for atom bombs."

"Aha! The atom bomb."

"Of course. The stone statue that comes for Don Giovanni, impious hedonist, is Mao, who appears to the cynical banqueting Western world and warns it with the bomb. . . ."

The meal was over. Mao's statue never came. (But, alas, China is full of these statues.) Then we had the odd sensation that we ought to run out of the restaurant as soon as possible, like customers who didn't have the money to pay. We knew perfectly well that we had been invited and that those who had invited us and served us had been extremely polite and courteous, genuinely pleased to have us appreciate the national dish. But, through no fault of theirs, we felt a sense of guilt. "Let's get out of here," I said, "before the waitress comes back."

And we left, or rather, we ran away. We hurried down the stairs two steps at a time, passed through the melancholy foyer, with its two red sofas and two large gilded mirrors, and went out into the crowded street. The car was waiting. We got in and drove off.

"We've committed a great sin," I said, "and now it's weighing on our bourgeois capitalist consciences."

"We had an exquisite dinner. And now it is resting lightly and so well on the stomachs of two people who, like any others, are always ready to appreciate the good things in life."

THE CHALLENGE OF HONG KONG

"Are these the same Chinese," I asked Dacia, "that we saw parading in Peking a few days ago, with flags, pictures of Mao, and the little red books of the sayings of Mao?"

"The same. Not the same individuals, but the same in the sense that they are also the Chinese people."

"Then it's been proved that one can do whatever one likes with people. Or that people can do anything they like with themselves."

"Let's say that men can do anything they choose with themselves."

We were staying in a hotel in Kowloon, the continental section of the island of Hong Kong. The area was completely Chinese, for the Europeans all live on the

island. From our window on the twentieth floor we had
a view of a residential building, a skyscraper, just across
the way. It was very near; between it and our hotel
there was a bare cement courtyard scattered with rot-
ting garbage. From our window we could see how small
the apartments were—just one or two rooms, and as
small as cells. It must have been suffocating to live in
such close quarters. In some of the rooms, beds were
set into the wall, one above the other like berths on a
train. It was close to evening, but many of the occu-
pants, unemployed or indolent, lay on the beds with
their backs to the windows, almost protruding from
them as a matter of fact, as if this exposure to the
outside air would provide some relief from the sultry
tropical humidity. Men in underwear and naked children moved slowly and with difficulty about the small,
crowded rooms. Women in black pajamas stood cooking
in front of minuscule stoves. These were poor people,
though perhaps less poor than the people of Canton and
Peking. But they had been uprooted from the country
of their origin and crowded together here. There had
been no real transplantation into another culture. They
had been set on the naked rock of a mercantile and
colonial metropolis of four million inhabitants. As if to
say that these families, teeming in promiscuous and
anguished cohabitation in that building, shared (or
pretended to share) the same view of the world as the
bankers, merchants, industrialists, and millionaires
whose beautiful, spacious villas, deep in luxurious subtropical gardens, we had seen the day before, during

a tour of the residential areas on the hills of Hong Kong.

"They're Communists, for the most part," Dacia said. "The elevator operators and bellboys almost fought over the copies of the French and English translations of the sayings of Mao that we brought from China."

"There are non-Communists too, who have fled here from China. Like our driver yesterday, who drove an American ambulance during the civil war between the Nationalists and the Communists. He's afraid he'll be put against a wall and shot if the Chinese ever invade Hong Kong."

"Capitalism has had several effects," I went on. "The most obvious one is that it has put men and objects on the same level. And often it leads to the production of objects that have a nicer, more finished, more attractive, more beautiful aspect than the men who produce and consume them. Maybe that is the origin of the French *nouveau roman's* idea that objects have an importance of their own independent of man and that man today has been transformed into an object like any other, perhaps an object that is less central and important than others. In fact, in capitalist countries it is often the case that clothes are much better-looking than the people who wear them, automobiles are much more impressive than their drivers, and houses are much more imaginative than their tenants. Let's go out on the hotel terrace and take a look at Hong Kong, a city that is certainly infinitely more beautiful than the people, rich and poor, who live here."

We went up to the roof garden of the hotel. Hong Kong is beautiful, very beautiful, with a beauty that reminds one a little of New York, the way the beauty of a younger sister sometimes recalls that of an older sister. It was sunset, and the sky above us was already green and hazy while the horizon was still red. The hills, darkened by the shadows of evening and swollen with impure and delirious subtropical vegetation, were the backdrop for close-set groups of white skyscrapers, straight, pure, spiritual, already sparkling and bejeweled with lighted windows. The city was before us, forming a semicircle all around the bay, which at that time of day was a gloomy blue, a hard, mineral, gemlike blue, chipped with purple highlights. The outlines of countless ships in the harbor, black as India ink, stood out against the lighter background of sea and sky: the enormous shapes of transatlantic liners, the long low forms of oilers, the tall, solid figures of mercantile ships, the barely emerging tops of submarines, and the slender, pointed lines of war ships. Moving in and out among these motionless black forms were the equally dark forms of pudgy tugboats with tall and slender smokestacks, and sampans, like small medieval craft with the curved edges of their prows and decks. I had a long look at this marvelous panorama, and then I remarked, "Hong Kong is a rejuvenated city."

"Rejuvenated, how?"

"When I was here more than thirty years ago, it was a Victorian derelict. Do you remember the post office, a runt squashed between two giant white skyscrapers, a long low building of brick the color of ox-blood and darkened by damp—a neo-Gothic building? Well, all Hong Kong used to be like that. The English lived on the hills in Edwardian stucco villas, and the Chinese were crowded in back of the port in sordid, crumbling caravansaries bridled with collapsing balconies and crooked verandas. There were some banks in Empire style, nineteenth-century structures of shiny dark granite that had a kind of sinister respectability. And that's all. I tell you, Hong Kong has been rejuvenated."

Hong Kong has in fact been transformed from a British colonial, mercantile city into a neocapitalist, American-style metropolis. The origin of this transformation is rather curious and deserves some comment.

About twenty years ago the French photographer Cartier-Bresson published a volume of photographs of China. It was the year of Mao's triumph. Among the many photographs was one that struck me as particularly expressive and eloquent. It had been taken on the eve of the entry of the Communist troops into Shanghai and showed a row of men and women in a strange state of panic, frenzied and controlled at the same time. They had rushed breathlessly to the banks to withdraw their savings to hide them before the arrival of Mao's troops. The photograph impressed me as a first-hand document of what happens when an invasion is imminent. Once people gathered up all their possessions into a bundle. Nowadays people withdraw their bank accounts. The world doesn't change much. But in that line of people crushed against each other, their tense faces avid and anxious, one could distinguish something more than the fear of losing their money, and this something else does not emerge so very often.

It was the sense of terror that is aroused not so much by the threat of material ruin as by the collapse of the scale of values one has lived by. In a few hours these values would cease to be; they would be violently and radically replaced by Maoist Communism. The Communist invasion was not just one more invasion, however bloody, after which one could go back to one's usual habitats and activities. It was the invasion of the "other," of the "different," of something that would never again allow a turning back. It was similar to such events, alas unphotographed, as the entry of the Turks into Christian Constantinople or the Spanish into pre-Columbian Mexico. The photograph documented an irreparable overthrow, something radical and final.

And yet, strange to say, it is to those unfortunate Chinese savers of Shanghai that Hong Kong owes its prosperity and rejuvenation. I mean this in a metaphorical sense, of course. Those small savers that Cartier-Bresson photographed, if they managed to escape, are now part of the throng of poor people in Hong Kong: dealers of all kinds, shopkeepers, prostitutes, salesmen. The people who changed the face of Hong Kong are the very rich *compradores,* usurers, warlords, landlords. They didn't line up in front of bank windows. They didn't flee in panic. With a telephone call or two, they had their capital transferred from Shanghai to Singapore, Tokyo, Formosa, and Hong Kong. They rejoined their capital in comfort, by plane, with their wives, concubines, children, servants, cooks, and major-domos. This does not change the fact that the terror Cartier-

Bresson photographed was universally experienced, by the small savers as well as the great usurers. And the link between this terror and Hong Kong's rejuvenation is, paradoxically, the seemingly simple but psychologically complex financial operation known as investment. Hong Kong owes its renewal to the transfusion into its old colonial veins of a vast amount of so-called "overseas Chinese" capital. That is, for the most part, of capital taken out of China at the time of Mao's victory.

It is a significant paradox of history that a defeated and deteriorated regime often recovers its firmness and strength, not in the calm of favorable conditions, but face to face with mortal danger. To the challenge of Mao's Communism, which has temporarily halted its advance in the outlying areas of Hong Kong, Chinese neocapitalism has replied with the challenge of financial investment in a city that everyone considered lost. I have used the term "challenge," but one could as easily speak of a "throw of the dice," a card played at great risk, a bluff, a gamble. And it may be more exact to say a challenge that is in fact unconscious, biological rather than historical. Historical awareness, or at least the belief of possessing it, is all on the other side of the border, in Mao's China. In Hong Kong one is faced with the same obscure impulse that drives a vine up a wall and a tree to extend its branches to the sun over a wall. In this sense, and in this sense only, can one speak of a challenge between Hong Kong and Mao's China. They are like two extremes facing each other in maximum essentiality and purity. On one side everything is willed, programmatic, conscious. On the other, everything is involuntary, spontaneous, unconscious.

Overseas Chinese capitalism's challenge to Mao's Communism is based on this simple train of thought: "Yes, all it would take is a single cannon shot from the Communists, and the English, who would like nothing better than to get rid of this colony too, would get out as fast as they could. But the Communists will not fire that cannon shot. Not just because it is convenient for them that Hong Kong, the only modernly equipped Chinese port, remain open to world trade, but because if Hong Kong were not there the Communists would have to invent a Hong Kong, create another port like it, run, organized, and administered by foreign intermediaries to handle China's enormous trade with the capitalist countries without risking political compromise."

This reasoning has permitted the extraordinary development of the port of Hong Kong, which ranks fifth in the world. At the root of this reasoning there is a complex network of faith and trust, as there always is where money is concerned: Chinese capitalists' faith in the English (and recent events have shown that this faith is not unfounded); the English faith in Mao's China (now profoundly shaken); Mao's China's faith in itself (stronger than ever). These various trusts created the present equilibrium of Hong Kong's position. This equilibrium has not been destroyed but it has been seriously compromised by the Chinese attempt to transform the English colony into another Macao, that is, a colonial port in which, however, the colonialist power is, in a manner of speaking, a vassal of China. In Macao this state of vassalage has finally been accepted by Portugal. In Hong Kong, on the other hand, the unconscious challenge of overseas Chinese capitalism has been increased by the totally unconscious English refusal to follow Portugal's example.

We were on one of the main streets of Kowloon. There were Indian shops in which the salesmen wore turbans and white jackets and chiefly sold Madras cottons; English stores selling books, woollens, shoes, men's shirts, ready-made clothes, and sporting goods; Japanese shops with cameras, transistors, toys, lacquerwork, and ceramics; Chinese shops dealing in curios, antiques, porcelain, bric-a-brac, and souvenirs; American shops with checkered shirts, windbreakers, blue jeans, and moccasins; French shops selling perfumes and French fashions; Malayan, Philippine, German, Persian, and Arabian shops; shops of every shape and kind. And between the shops were Chinese, European, Japanese, Korean, and Polynesian restaurants, bars of all kinds, cellar nightclubs, tea houses, currency exchanges, strip-tease halls, cinemas, and pinball machine parlors. And on the upper floors were Turkish baths, massage establishments, beauty centers, hair-dressers, photographic studios, and, of course, albeit unseen, houses of ill-repute, the mythological *maisons de rendezvous* described in one of Robbe-Grillet's cinematographic novels. And there were travel agencies, tourist bureaus, airline and shipping offices, import and export offices. And more. There were trade displays of motorboats, automobiles, bicycles, motorcycles, sewing machines, and typewriters, as well as showcases of china, electric appliances of every kind, hardware, kitchen appliances, surgical instruments, tobacco, and pastry. And every now and then there were huge department stores several stories tall where one could buy anything, and one could see the staircases and counters and the crowd through the window panes. The list could be extended. It ought to be extended in the form of a catalogue. That is the only way to express the feeling one has when walking along the streets of Hong Kong, a feeling of being in a city in which all there is are things to buy and sell, and buyers and sellers. In fact, a sales catalogue more than a thousand pages long, on lightweight paper, with lists of merchandise and prices, and a brief word of commendation—a catalogue is really the only, shall I say, literary composition that can give an adequate idea of Hong Kong. Even the austere Chinese People's Republic has accepted this atmosphere. There is a huge ten-story emporium with the modest products of Communist China and immense pictures of Mao in the windows. If Hong Kong represents a capitalist challenge to Chinese Communism, then it is also true that with this department store Mao's China challenges itself. The extremes of this cycle of buying and selling are represented by the American Marines and the child prostitutes, perhaps actually children, in the buttoned jacket with a stiff, 1930's Shanghai-style collar, miniskirt split to the hip, their faces poorly powdered, their red mouths, and their innocent and shadowed slanted eyes. They are the absolute in sellers, because they are selling themselves. And the giant Marines with their huge shoulders and small shaved heads and their rolling walk are the absolute buyers—they buy everything. Sometimes the two extremes meet, in an embrace in some lurid hotel that lets rooms by the hour. We saw the little girl, happy as could be that she had sold herself, hurrying off on the arm of the American colossus, who seemed highly pleased with his purchase. Most of the time, however, one notices no single particular occurrence, no individual happening. We were dazed and stunned by the delirious swarm of offers, invitations, allurements, and enticements of consumption. It was the same atmosphere one sees in certain shopping areas of New York, London, and Paris. But here it was all business, with a charge of violence and obsessiveness that one is not aware of in other cities.

Not all situations of conflict are situations of challenge, however. It is not true, for example, that nations with Communist regimes are "always" hostile to those with capitalist regimes. It is true, however, that some Communist nations are hostile, for reasons having nothing to do with political ideology, to certain capitalist nations. Which amounts to saying that coexistence is possible, that such hostility is not due to the fact that coexistence is impossible. There is undoubtedly conflict between Italy and Yugoslavia, for example, but there is no challenge. There is, as I have mentioned, a challenge between Hong Kong and Mao's China, or rather, between Mao's China and the whole world. And in

Hong Kong the challenge between the world and Mao's China is more intransigent than anywhere else.

What does this challenge consist of? I should say that it consists precisely in the fact that the two conflicting situations are typical and extreme at the same time. Hong Kong has all the characteristics of capitalism, yet not one of the characteristics sometimes shared by capitalism and Communism. In Hong Kong, the traditional modifications of capitalist abstraction are missing: the soil and the peasants, a nation and a national culture, religion and religious tradition. Hong Kong is a pitiless example of what money by itself achieves, that is, pure consumption, with no justification but profit. Mao's China has so far not modified nor seemed disposed to modify Communist abstraction with the concessions (which it considers revisionism) which are by now habitual in other Communist countries, concessions to individual liberty and well-being. On the contrary, the Cultural Revolution has confirmed and reinforced the absolute lack of such correctives. Thus Hong Kong lives for profit and consumption. And in Mao's China consumption has been reduced to the absolute minimum and profit has been abolished. There are two challenges, then, and, as I have said, they are extreme. At the same time, they are in a sense more biological than political and economic. At the level of the struggle for life, everything becomes essential and extreme. And there is no further possibility of compromise, even when, as is the case of Hong Kong and Mao's China, a sort of compromise is temporarily maintained by both sides.

ARE THE COMMUNISTS REALLY THERE?

Anyone traveling the route of airports from Seoul, Korea, by way of Tokyo and perhaps Manila, to Taipeh and Hong Kong, maybe Kuala Lumpur and of course Saigon, and as far as Bangkok, witnesses an impressive phenomenon, the overflowing or flooding of East Asia by the Americans. The United States and Asia are separated by the Pacific Ocean, but it is as if there were only an easily negotiated creek. The Americans have committed themselves in this part of the world, and their commitment is not merely military but, in the broadest sense, cultural.

Militarily, the United States, by means of smaller or larger armies (Formosa, South Korea, Vietnam, Thailand), alliances (Australia, New Zealand, the Philippines, Hong Kong), and community of interests (Japan, Indonesia, Malaya), controls all eastern Asia. As for the cultural flood . . . I shall merely note that in any invasion the invader offers, gives, and imposes his own culture on the invaded. But, fatally and unconsciously, he in turn receives, accepts, and adopts the culture of the invaded. I repeat, it is fatal, and I mean fatal in its original tragic sense. If, instead of invading one of the oldest civilizations in the world, the Americans had invaded, let us say, Borneo, they soon would have become "Borneanized," without choosing to be so and completely unawares. What has here been received and adopted, however unconsciously, by these athletic, hypernourished, and infantile soldiers, the blond, languid, and deodorized women, and the wild, virtually albino children that crowd the hotels of these cities, pass through the airports, and fill the airplanes that fly from one city to another?

On a conscious level, one knows why the Americans are in Asia. Because of their obsession with and hatred of Communism. When I speak of "Communism" in connection with the cause of the American war of "containment," I am not referring—that is clear—to actual, objective Communism, the Communism of Marx, Lenin, and probably Stalin. No, I am speaking of something mythological and at the same time worn-out, explosive and inconsistent—in short, something very much like that other something, "imperialism," so often spoken of in countries that consider themselves America's enemies. Clearly Communism and imperialism are two realities, and clearly we live a world split by these two realities. At the same time, however, the words "Communism" and "imperialism" now stand not for the objective realities but for the feelings of the people who make use of these words—that is, for something imprecise, vague, deceptive, illusory, and unreal.

The Americans are in Asia to stand up to Communism. At the same time they are receiving something from the Asians that in future is bound to correct, modify, and profoundly enhance the American way of life. What will this correction, modification, and enhancement consist of? It might be said that it is already a great corrective to have seen Communism with one's own eyes, to have touched it with one's hand. But Communism is not all there is in Asia. Before Communism there were other, perhaps even more important, beliefs. At this point what is required is an irrational flight, something my nature is incapable of—prophecy. So I shall limit myself to indicating, by way of example, some of the effects on the United States of the Japanese war and of the occupation of Japan. Japanese culture, Japanese taste, Japanese customs, and the Japanese view of the world have been absorbed to a larger degree than one might think by Anglo-Saxon, Puritan America. And perhaps the war with Japan and the occupation were but the first stages of this fatal flooding of Asia by America, of this marriage born out of hate and love, of this symbiosis or attempted symbiosis . . .

These were my thoughts as I drove across Seoul,

among the pits and mounds and puddles of public construction work, as numerous as they are inefficient,
toward Panmunjom and the North Korean border. I
was accompanied by a South Korean functionary, ami-
able, smiling, and polished, and incredibly, tenaciously,
inflexibly optimistic. "There's no end to Seoul," I said.
"The center is small but the city is immense. The
suburbs begin in the center and go on forever."

"It was the center of a city of three hundred thousand
inhabitants until very recently." He smiled. "The emperors built gardens and palaces here. Then the Japanese put up some public buildings and a few hotels.
Then with the war we were inundated by immigration
from the country. Today Seoul has four million inhabitants."

"What do they do? How do they live? Is Seoul rich?
Is there much industry in Seoul?"

"No, it isn't rich, and there is little industry." He continued to smile. "But it will become rich and wo shall
create industry. All these people came from the country
to work and to progress. We'll make them work and
progress."

Work and progress? I looked at the streets we passed,
rows of huts, sheds with tiny shops and enormous signs
and minuscule windows, every now and then a larger
house, old and peeling, or a nice-looking modern building; the sidewalks jammed with rushing throngs; a
torrent of automobiles of all kinds slowly streaming
between the pits and mounds of public construction
work. "There are metropolises formed by a concentration

of wealth, managerial groups, factories, and products," I remarked. "And there are metropolises formed by extra-economic causes, like wars, rural unemployment, the need for protection, and so on. Except in Japan, the first are almost all Western and the second are almost all Asian. Seoul seems to me to belong to the second category."

My companion smiled. "We'll see to it that Seoul passes into the first category as soon as possible."

"But all the industries and raw materials are in North Korea."

"We're organizing industry now. Switzerland didn't have raw materials either, but it's become an industrial country."

Switzerland? I looked at the rugged hills, rocky and bare and altogether too shiny, genuine Asian hills, at the bottom of which Seoul, like muddy water on flooded land, was spreading out of its original valley into the surrounding dales and valleys, and I said, "The average per capita income of South Korea is $108, that of the Chinese People's Republic is $120, and that of Japan is $800. Which do you expect to reach—the Chinese or the Japanese norm?"

"The Japanese, of course."

"I should say that Japan is still a long way off."

"It is. But think about these figures."

"What figures?"

"Between 1960 and 1963 there was an overall annual rise of ten percent in production. This was the result of our five-year plan of economic development. Do you know how much industrial production, for example, has risen in a year? Eighteen percent."

"I'm not in any position to evaluate those figures. I must rather trust what I see. Korea gives the impression, at least for now, of being a poor and underdeveloped country, overwhelmingly agricultural, with an enormous and chaotic capital whose population seems to have a rather low standard of living."

"It is low, but it will rise."

We were in the country now. In the city one could see the effects of the war, but in the country one could see the war itself, or rather the unhealthy, peculiar situation which an armistice that has lasted fifteen years is. A light rain was falling on the bright green countryside from a sky swollen with low and motionless black clouds. We proceeded at a snail's pace behind a column of armored trucks. They were full of troops. The soldiers stood in double file with their helmets over their eyes; they were leaning forward and were looking at us but they probably didn't see us. We too were part of this waking dream that is Korea, Asia— American intervention in Korea and Asia. At a turn in the road the column poured through the sentry-guarded entrance of a camp surrounded by barbed wire. We saw row after row of motor-drawn cannon and armored cars painted green, with a white star. The prefabricated barracks were painted green, and everywhere soldiers were coming and going. We drove past and finally picked up speed.

"How many American soldiers are stationed in Korea?" I asked my guide.

"Fifty thousand," he answered with a smile.

"How many soldiers are there in the South Korean Army?"

"The South Korean Army has six hundred thousand soldiers." He paused for a moment and then added, "It is one of the strongest in the world."

"How many troops do you have in Vietnam?"

"Forty-five thousand."

"Has North Korea sent troops to help North Vietnam?"

"China wanted it to, but North Korea refused."

"How do you know that China wanted it to and that North Korea refused?"

"The North Korean government was suddenly attacked in the poster newspapers in Peking."

I left it at that. Korea is a kind of Asian Poland. Chinese influence, Russian influence, American influence, and English influence have warred in this country for centuries. The result, at least for now, is the division of Korea in two. The automobile drove on. We passed a line of American soldiers. They walked slowly in the rain, single file, along the edge of the road. Most of them were tall, lanky, and blond. There were a few short dark ones too, Italian Americans or Puerto Ricans, and every now and then a Negro. They looked at us out of the corners of their eyes, bored, indifferent. We sped on. We saw tanks. I don't know why but they reminded me of the combat elephants of antiquity: the same enormous bulks, slow, towering, surmounted by the tiny head of the driver, indifferent and almost inhuman, insensitive in any case to what the bulk could roll over and crush. And the same trunks, or forward cannon, protruding menacingly.

Several miles farther, we reached a broad river that gradually unfolded as we approached an iron bridge: broad bends of brown, muddy-colored water, with low marshy banks to the south and steep rocky banks to the north. All about it was an air of solitude, of nature depopulated, a desert. One thought at once of the war (in Korea one thinks constantly of the war) that had halted on these banks, awaiting the reconstruction of destroyed bridges. It was a river of military disaster, of invasion or retreat. The bridge was narrow and entirely of iron. In the dimness of the rain, the American sentries patrolled up and down the bridge. Other sentries stood at the end of the bridge at the checkpoint.

"So many precautions," I remarked to the guide.

"To prevent Communist infiltration."

"Is there a lot of it?"

"They cross the river by night and by day too. If you look over there, you can see American patrols in the cane brake. What do you think? It is because of infiltration that there has been a curfew in Seoul for thirteen years."

I didn't think anything, I was there to look. The car set off again through the green countryside soaking in rain, under the black spring sky, in the sharp odor of acacia in bloom. Finally we reached the demilitarized zone. A sign in English gave notice of this, alongside a kind of small, Korean-style arch of triumph. The car was now crossing a slightly different landscape. First there had been fields, rice paddies, cultivated land. Now there was nothing but expanses of vegetation and woods gone wild. And everywhere a sense of abandonment. The guide spoke. "This is the demilitarized zone. Nobody lives or works here. It's gone wild. And do you know what? The game has increased, because no one hunts."

"What game?"

"Roe deer, wild rabbit, pheasant. Look, look . . ."

I looked and saw two roe deer chasing each other over the grass, free and happy. Farther away, in a clearing, two pheasants hopped from one foot to another and then rose in flight. "It's like the Garden of Eden," I remarked. "No people, no cultivation, just weeds and free animals."

He smiled his approval. "Yes, the Garden of Eden."

We had arrived at the point from which the war tourists set off. Yes, war tourists, because the Americans—partly for reasons of propaganda and partly because of their innate didactic inclination—have transformed the armistice boundary into a tourist and educational attraction, like Niagara Falls or the geysers of the Rocky Mountains. One visits the border to look at North Korea in the same way that one goes to look at a natural wonder. Buses take groups of Koreans or Westerners, and automobiles take individual visitors, like myself. We went into a long low prefabricated building where we were received by an American major in uniform. He was to be our guide now, he was to make the explanations, this Virgil of that little Korean limbo. He asked us to be seated and took a pointer with which he directed our attention to some placards on an easel, and in fifteen minutes he had told us the history of the armistice zone. We sat through the toneless, slow, quiet explanation, scientific in style and occasionally relieved by delicate humor, just like a lecture in an American college.

We left the building and drove toward the border. It had stopped raining. The acacias dripped on our heads as we got out of the car and started walking along a muddy road toward a lookout point. There was a small platform there, and the major asked us to step up to it. From it we could see the vast panorama of valleys and hills, apparently altogether depopulated.

"The Communists are down there," the major told us.

A florid, heavily made up American girl who had joined our group along with two or three of her friends asked, as she chewed gum frenetically: "Where?"

"Down there, behind that clump of trees."

"Are the Communists there?"

"Yes, the Communists are there."

"Really?"

"Yes, really."

"I can't see them."

"There is a village, but it's hidden by the hill."

"A Communist village?"

"Yes, a Communist village."

"Are all the inhabitants Communists?"

"Yes, they are all Communists."

There was a deep silence. The major added indifferently, "They could shoot at us. They do sometimes."

From the platform we went over to where the two armistice commissions had been meeting every day for fourteen years. It was an open space between the green, flowering hills. In the open space, to one side, there was a small commemorative building, Korean-style, in the soft bright colors of Sicilian ice cream. On the other side was a row of prefabricated barracks, some painted blue, others green. The green ones were North Korean, the blue were South Korean. The major explained. "The demarcation line passes between the barracks and runs right through the middle of the table at which the two commissions sit. If you like, you can have a look at one of the meetings. I mean, you can look through the window. I think there is a meeting going on now."

He waved us to follow him, and we went up to the largest of the blue barracks and pressed our noses against a window pane, like poor folk peering in at a party. And in a long low room we saw a green table that divided the room in two. The North Koreans were sitting on one side, dressed in olive drab, with red badges, and hard, rigid, serious, hostile faces. On the other side were the Americans and the South Koreans—two South Koreans in uniform, no less hostile and serious, and an American officer in a military shirt with the sleeves rolled up. He was a big blond man, with blond forearms and a blond chest. The two commissions seemed to be discussing something. I could see the mouths and hands move, but I heard nothing.

The girl with the chewing gum asked, "What do they talk about?"

"It depends on the day. Some days they talk about nonsense, like the removal of boundary stakes at night."

"What stakes?"

"They use stakes to mark the border. The North Koreans come and move the stakes at night. And the next day we put them back where they were. This is one of the things the two commissions discuss."

"And if not that?"

"Well, yesterday a mine blew up one of the American barracks. Two men were killed. But the mine won't be discussed for a few days yet, if it is discussed at all."

"Are there many incidents like that to be discussed?"

"So far we have accused the North Koreans of 5,300 armistice violations. They have accused us of 42,311 violations. We have acknowledged eighty-nine, and the North Koreans have acknowledged two."

"How long have the commissions been meeting?"

"They've been meeting every day for fourteen years."

"Fourteen years?"

"Yes. We're at war. Armistice doesn't mean there is peace. It just means there is no fighting."

"And when will there be peace?"

"Who knows? Maybe never."

We watched for a long time, pressing our faces against

the glass. Then suddenly the two commissions rose, exchanged military salutes, turned their backs on each other, and went out. We hurried to the rear door, where the North Koreans were leaving. It had started to rain again. We saw the North Koreans leave the barracks and walk slowly off in the rain.

The girl asked eagerly, "Are they the Communists?"

"Yes, they're Communists." The major was silent for a moment, and then he said, "I could show you a cage of homing pigeons over there, in North Korean territory. They say they've been trained to fly only over the green barracks—the Communist ones—and to avoid the blue, capitalist barracks." He paused for a moment to judge the effect this had on us. Then he added, "But I won't take you there, because it isn't true. It's a proven fact that pigeons can't distinguish colors. Anyway, it's raining. Let's go eat."